BREAKING IT DOWN

BREAKING IT DOWN

Audition Techniques for Actors of the Global Majority

Nicole Hodges Persley
Monica White Ndounou

ROWMAN & LITTLEFIELD
Lanham • Boulder • New York • London

Published by Rowman & Littlefield
An imprint of The Rowman & Littlefield Publishing Group, Inc.
4501 Forbes Boulevard, Suite 200, Lanham, Maryland 20706
www.rowman.com

6 Tinworth Street, London SE11 5AL, United Kingdom

British Library Cataloguing in Publication Information Available

Library of Congress Cataloging-in-Publication Data

Names: Hodges Persley, Nicole, 1969– author. | Ndounou, Monica White, 1976– author.
Title: Breaking it down : audition techniques for actors of the global majority / Nicole Hodges
    Persley, Monica White Ndounou.
Description: Rowman & Littlefield, [2021] | Includes bibliographical references and index. |
    Summary: "This volume offers strategic approaches to auditioning for women, men, and
    non-binary actors of the global majority. It provides a fresh approach from the perspec-
    tives of two directors of color who are also actors working in theater, film, and televi-
    sion."—Provided by publisher.
Identifiers: LCCN 2020052284 (print) | LCCN 2020052285 (ebook) | ISBN 9781538137079
    (cloth) | ISBN 9781538137086 (epub)
Subjects: LCSH: Auditions—United States. | Minorities in the performing arts—Vocational
    guidance—United States. | Acting—Vocational guidance—United States.
Classification: LCC PN2071.A92 H57 2021 (print) | LCC PN2071.A92 (ebook) | DDC
    792.02/8—dc23
LC record available at https://lccn.loc.gov/2020052284
LC ebook record available at https://lccn.loc.gov/2020052285

In loving memory of Cicely Tyson

CONTENTS

INTRODUCTION

Actors at every career level can experience what the late, great actor, director, and writer Chadwick Boseman described during his keynote address at the 150th commencement of his alma mater, the historically Black college Howard University, in 2018.[1] The speech laid out his early process of "breaking it down" to land and perform roles and how he avoided being broken down by an entertainment industry that insists on stereotyping Black people and other marginalized groups.

In the latter half of his speech, Boseman primarily addressed his experience as a cisgender, Black man and actor building his early career. He shared some of the triumphs and challenges of his early career and how they laid the foundation for his career path, which was grounded in fulfilling his purpose. His story speaks volumes about the challenges actors of the global majority face in theater, film, and television:

> I was on a roll when I entered the system of entertainment: theater, television, and film. In my first New York audition for a professional play, I landed the lead role. From that play I got my first agent. From that agent I got an onscreen audition. It was a soap opera. It wasn't *Third Watch*. It was a soap opera on a major network. I scored that role too. I felt like Mike Tyson

when he first came on the scene, knocking out opponents in the first round.

Boseman's early success in auditions helped him land an agent and gave him the confidence and exposure he needed to access opportunities on stage and screen. Although he does not name the soap opera in the speech, it has been identified as *All My Children*, a popular soap opera that ran on network television from 1970 to 2013—a pretty big break for any new actor.

As he discovered the differences in process and preparation in theater versus television, he learned other valuable lessons. He went on:

> With this soap opera gig I was already promised to make six figures, more money than I had ever seen. I was feelin' myself. But once I got the first script, and with soap operas, you very often get the script the night before and you shoot the whole episode in one day with little to no time to prepare. Once I saw the role I was playing, I found myself conflicted. The role wasn't necessarily stereotypical, "a young man in his formative years with a violent streak pulled into the allure of gang involvement." That's somebody's real story.

What Boseman attempted to distinguish there is the fine line between stereotypes and believable, three-dimensional stories. Stereotypes are things that are often somebody's real story, yet become stereotypes because they are exaggerated assumptions that are projected onto the story of everyone in a certain group. Stereotypes are not fairytales, yet are often used by Hollywood as tales that represent a group as a whole, which is problematic and hurtful.

Boseman was right, of course, that a young man with a violent streak may find gang involvement alluring, regardless of what he looks like. At the same time, it does conform to a stereotype with someone who looks like him in a two-dimensional role. An actor facing such a breakdown has a choice to make. Boseman recognized the humanity in the character breakdown while also noting the potential harm in superficial treatment of the subject matter (gang involvement) and the character. In order to reconcile this conflict, Boseman referred back to his training at Howard University, which enabled him to immerse himself in Black culture and the performing arts under the tutelage of luminaries like Phylicia Rashad and Al Freeman Jr. He continued:

> Never judge the characters you play. That's what we were always taught. That's the first rule of acting: that any role played honestly can be empowering. But I was conflicted because this role seemed to be wrapped up in assumptions about us, as Black folk. The writing failed to search for specificity. Plus, there was barely a glimpse of positivity or talent in the character. Barely a glimpse of hope. I would have to make something out of nothing. I was conflicted. Howard had instilled in me a certain amount of pride and, for my taste, this role didn't live up to those standards.

Boseman went on to describe his interactions with show executives, which ended up getting him fired from the job, not because he was incapable and unskilled. He was let go because he asked probing questions about the character and circumstances, and his agent called to let him know that the executives "decided to go another way." Boseman knew, however, that he had to ask those complex questions in order to do his job as an actor. He could only hope that he had, in his words, "paved the way for a less stereotypical portrayal for the black actor that stepped into the role after me."[2] As it turned out, that Black actor was Boseman's eventual *Black Panther* (2018) castmate, Michael B. Jordan. Boseman's questioning had exposed some of the limitations of the writing, yet Jordan later confirmed that his own experience in the role also informed his subsequent choices to pass on stereotypical roles.

We know from our own HBCU experience at Spelman College that immersion in Black culture and performance, which affirmed our humanity and power, is vital to finding ways to break it down instead of being broken down. Through our training and acting experiences at Spelman and with other Black acting teachers and directors, we also developed criteria for assessing roles and approaches to the craft along with strategies for navigating a system that has historically devalued our humanity and distorted the range and depth of people and cultures our bodies can represent in story-telling. *Breaking It Down* shares some of those strategies, those specifically focused on auditioning, while also encouraging further study of the craft of acting by providing selected insights in each chapter and a list of resources that can help you get started or build up your existing career. And it all starts with you.

TWENTY-FIRST-CENTURY AUDITION TECHNIQUES

Breaking It Down: Audition Techniques for Actors of the Global Majority is drawn from the idea of "breaking it down" as a play on the actual breaking down of scripts that actors do and the break-down services casting directors use to identify actors for auditions. In African American vernacular English (AAVE), to "break it down" in conversation is to clarify a topic at length by making it plain or discussing it in the simplest terms. In hip hop, to "break it down" in dance or music is to feel the beat and express through movement and/or the beat with emphatic intention. This book is designed to help artists of the global majority achieve three key objectives: Break it down! Bring it! Book it! Actors can achieve these objectives in ten steps.

We recommend you do the steps in the order we provide them, but, as celebrated Black casting director Robi Reed Humes has said, "You have to do what is good for you. What you can live with, go home with. If it sits well in your spirit do it. If you don't get it right the first time, do it again. Try to leave the room doing it how you want to do it."[3] *Breaking It Down* is designed to help you!

WHY THIS BOOK?

We wrote this book because, quite frankly, we needed it. We needed a book that captured many of the things that we share with students in our classes and actors in our productions. Learning some key steps to establishing a solid audition process and finding an acting approach that works for you is key to your success. Our goal is to open opportunities for actors, with and without training, along with teachers and directors to gain access to the entertainment industry. The principal audience for this book is students at the community college, college, and university levels that are preparing for a career in the professional theater and entertainment industry.

This book is unique in that it presents audition strategies that are rooted in theater performance and then connects those skillsets to television and film acting processes. We make suggestions of how actors of the global majority can address industry biases, stereotypes, and other work conditions to develop strategies to become self-reflexive, affirmed, and prepared to book professional performance work. Specifically, instead of encouraging actors of the global majority to "become universal," we encourage them to incorporate what makes them unique into their performances. The text is also unique in that we provide an insider's perspective, as we have a combined over twenty years of experience working across genres of theater, television, and film as both performers and directors. We aim for this to be the only book on the market that takes into consideration the racial, social, cultural, and gender identifications of the actor walking into the audition room and the existing stereotypes that actors of the global majority have to work against when they make their living in a predominantly White entertainment industry.

We see this book as a unique text in the audition book arena because most of the audition books on the market separate audition information by genre (theater or film and television) and consist of long narratives about the theory of auditioning, books of monologues from random one-act plays, or acting-for-the-camera books. This book brings all of these various areas together in one text with simple techniques and journal reflection prompts that apply to theater, film, and television work. The aforementioned texts are not bad, per se, but they do usually assume that the performer has acted before and require you to read a separate book for each area. This book can be used by actors with or without training, no matter the measure, from MFA to beginner, because this book is not intended to teach you *how* to act or to give you acting techniques.

The goal of the book is to offer you techniques that are synthesized from multiple acting approaches that center and affirm your identity while giving you a roadmap for more successful auditions that lead to booking jobs. Our primary focus is on auditioning in the United States, although some of the strategies may apply in other global markets. This book is not designed to help you solve that, but it may offer some insights on the need to do so as part of your practice. We hope that it will help give you the tools to become a self-reflexive actor who is proud of who they are despite the rampant racism, sexism, and classism in the entertainment industry.

Casting directors in the entertainment industry have a very difficult job because they have to serve as the human resource agents for production companies who decide to produce scripts and hire directors who may or may not have the cultural fluency to tell stories about people of the global majority. For non-White casting agents, the job of casting is even more complex because they are also charged with helping diversify an industry that has been, and continues to be, committed to perpetuating representations of people of the global majority that are racist and demeaning. For allied casting agents, the job of casting is difficult because they are asked to "find diverse talent," yet they are given scripts that may attempt to erase the racial and ethnic specificity of the experiences of non-White people. We want to stress that casting directors across racial lines have difficult jobs, and we want to help actors become prepared to ask informed questions, do research about the agencies that represent them, and research the projects they audition for so that they can partner with casting directors to be informed professionals who want to challenge the structural inequalities that are embedded in the foundations of the entertainment industry. We celebrate the casting directors who continue to challenge racist breakdowns, advocate for actors across racial lines, and stand for justice in the moments where the risk is high.

Not only do we celebrate casting directors who work from a social justice paradigm, but we also draw on our own experiences as actors, directors, and professors who train actors in universities, colleges, and regional theater and film environments where we direct. We have directed and helped train actors who have gone on to perform in Broadway shows, films, and network and streaming shows. We will tell you, as we have told them, things that most of the time no one says out loud because so much of actor training in formal training programs and teaching practice is centered in Whiteness. At the same time, actors who are not of the global majority will benefit greatly from using this book as well. Decentering Eurocentric approaches to acting can help all actors learn how to see the world around them with new eyes. Actors should be able to enter into a text with a point of empathy with the character they play. By learning the social injustices that colleagues of the global majority face in acting classes and the entertainment workplace every day, we hope that allies, accomplices, and coconspirators will be refreshed in their commitment to creating equitable and inclusive spaces on all theater, television, and film productions on stage and backstage. In front of the camera and behind it.

If a production you work on is all White, you have to ask yourself, *What's going on? Does this space reflect the world around me? How can we all be part of the solution for an equitable and inclusive entertainment industry?* Equity and inclusivity should happen not just in front of the house or the camera, but also behind the scenes. We need the industry to provide equity in all aspects of production from casting to hair and make-up. We hope this book will help many artists, casting directors, and directors (even agents and managers) make positive steps in the right direction toward inclusivity and retention of excellent talent of the global majority. Our breakdown technique can introduce you to audition techniques that can help you affirm yourself, become more empathetic toward others, and tune into your instincts as a person who is proficient in being human and portraying humanity.

KEY TERMS

We have chosen to use the terms *people/actors of the global majority* instead of *people/actors of color*. The terms *people of the global
majority* (PGM) and *actors of the global majority* (AGM) come
from the interdisciplinary terminology of environmental, cultural,
and Black studies. We use *people of the global majority* interchangeably with *black, indigenous, and people of color*, as Black,
Indigenous, Asian, and Pacific Islander people represent over 80
percent of the world's population.[4]

People of color lumps non-White people together in a way that
still centers Whiteness and avoids the particularities of the distinct
experiences of racial groups. The term also fails to acknowledge
how White supremacy thrives through bias like anti-Blackness per-
meating across racial groups. In fact, by lumping "people of color"
together, the term fails to acknowledge that White people are in the
minority globally, a fact that biased casting obscures across television, theater, and film.[5] The term *people of the global majority* also
nuances categorization that does not center race (what people look
like phenotypically but rather the fact that we are people, which
assumes associations with culture that are connected to race but not
defined exclusively by race).

Our text is focused primarily on auditioning for U.S.-based systems of entertainment, which are tied to a history of particular racial
categorizations, histories, and issues that may vary in an international context. Thus, we are not conflating actors of the global majority
in the United States with all actors sharing related ancestry and/or
phenotypical racial categorization and intersectional identities
throughout the world. As individuals and members of larger communities that are distinct, we acknowledge you. Yet we also recognize connections due to the ways bodies are read in the U.S. entertainment industry—specifically, the bodies of people of the global
majority, LGBTQIA+, or disabled, fat, thin, our bodies are frequently minimized or erased from predominantly White, cis, able-bodied
narratives or used interchangeably in ways that can complicate the

audition process and, as Boseman alluded to, the process of booking the role.

BREAKING IT DOWN

The steps and exercises in this book will help demystify the process of booking a job through the audition process. You will break down your process rather than being broken down by the process or the inequities that plague the entertainment industry. In this book, regardless of your career stage, you will learn how to break down the character using the character description in the script and/or the casting notice as the initial point of departure to determine if the role is of interest and aligns with your personal and professional goals and your skillsets. You will then learn how to breakdown the character as presented in the script and the sides from the script through a series of steps that guide your process of using the written text, research, and imagination to engage in a truthful performance in the audition. These steps acknowledge the various challenges actors of the global majority have faced historically as a very real part of the audition process. The journal prompts at the end of each chapter help empower the actor through self-knowledge and self-discovery, skilled script analysis and application, and preparedness for the range of encounters that can occur before and during an audition.

By focusing on breaking down the process of preparing for and performing in an audition, rather than being broken down by the system that complicates the audition process, we encourage you to center wellness as an integral part of the audition process and ultimately general practice as a working actor. Centering wellness in craft is particularly necessary for actors representing the global majority due to the harmful images that have misrepresented our people and cultures across multiple platforms for generations. By acknowledging this history in how you approach the audition process and encouraging you to trust in your abilities and potential to create and access alternative opportunities, we emphasize an abundance mentality rather than a scarcity one. Changing your mindset at the outset of the process can change the outcome because it increases your confidence and preparedness. You will take a cultivated approach to shaping your career through selected auditioning and role selection. Centering your purpose in building your legacy as an actor may require an entrepreneurial approach; you may have to create opportunities, rather than waiting for them to emerge.

Breaking It Down encourages actors representing a range of cultural backgrounds and identities to embrace every aspect of themselves and to consider auditioning as part of the process of building a career and legacy with longevity, even at the beginning of their careers. It is never too early to take yourself seriously as an actor when you are willing to do the work to be your very best. Preparing for opportunities in advance can go a long way in landing a callback, booking a role, and/or building a reputation and relationships with casting directors, directors, and agents.

When you learn how to break it down, you can truly "bring it" in the audition and the role itself. "Bring it," as a rallying cry for actors of the global majority, recognizes how frequently we are still too often called on to prove our humanity by erasing and minimizing our culture or only including those stereotypical elements made legible and popular through misrepresentation. *Breaking It Down* encourages actors of the global majority to bring their full selves into every audition, and our journal prompts will help you map your own process in order to bring it!

This approach is distinct from other audition texts that do not acknowledge how race, culture, and intersecting identities can collide with the audition process. We operate under the assumption of our humanity and yours, refusing to prove anything to anyone about who we are and what we can do as people of the global majority. Thus, we encourage self-knowledge and discovery and preparedness to engage with the character as written in the text (play, scripts, commercial copy, or any other text you use to audition). With your body as your instrument and your accumulated, varied ways of knowing as tools, you can build truthful performances through detailed preparation for the audition.

While our book focuses on how to help you book the job by breaking it down and bringing it in the audition, we provide resources that can help you further once you book the job or land the role. These resources offer additional insights on some of the skills, tools, and materials you may need to continue to build the character throughout the production and performance process. Additionally, industry insights embedded throughout each chapter will offer information that can prove useful in navigating the industry generally, particularly in consideration of auditioning.

Through the ten steps we describe in the following ten chapters, you will learn how to break down the character and script, developing or enhancing your audition process, which can be challenging for all actors at any career stage, but especially when starting out. Each chapter's journal prompts will enable you to respond to our call to audition with autonomy and self-assurance while helping you document your process for every audition through recognizable patterns that emerge in your journal entries. Each chapter helps you identify the pitfalls and barriers that may be keeping you from booking jobs. There are also recommended spreadsheet templates made accessible through our website. We encourage you to download these and use them to track your progress and maintain a record of the connections you are making as you audition. These elements, along with the lists of resources in the appendix, will become a part of your toolkit as an actor to support your growth, development, and professionalization as a creative entrepreneur of your acting career while you book jobs.

CHAPTER BREAKDOWN

- Chapter 1, "Establishing and Breaking Boundaries," centers wholeness and wellness in the process of establishing boundaries before, during, and after the audition.
- Chapter 2, "Tell the Truth," emphasizes the importance of being honest about your abilities, experience, and look with yourself and casting directors and directors.

- Chapter 3, "Read the Story, Not the Lines," focuses on the importance of reading the full story rather than just the lines in order to achieve a more holistic understanding of your role in the narrative.
- Chapter 4, "Play Punctuation and Practice Pronunciation," illustrates strategies for identifying clues for expected language use and the importance of studying and practicing cadence before the audition.
- Chapter 5, "Playing the Action," recognizes key elements of Stanislavsky-based training that emphasize the role of action in producing believable performances.
- Chapter 6, "Identifying the Emotions," reveals the relationship between playing actions and emotions as well as the potential use of acting traditions developed by people of the global majority as central or supplemental to audition practice.
- Chapter 7, "Understand the Social and Cultural Context Clues," maps the importance and practical application of researching history and culture and applying them to performance for an audition.
- Chapter 8, "Face Stereotypes," acknowledges the painful history and contemporary prevalence of stereotyping historically marginalized groups and offers strategies for combating and subverting them in performance should an actor elect to proceed with an audition that may be for a stereotypical role.
- Chapter 9, "Self-Tapes," provides tips and insights on how to produce self-tapes for auditions that will help you get callbacks.
- Chapter 10, "Agents and Managers," helps actors build professional relationships with agents, managers, and casting directors.
- The conclusion synthesizes the steps into a final reflection on how this book can help support the individual and collective well-being of communities of actors, particularly people of the global majority in the midst of the shifting tides of a historically inequitable and biased industry.

It is easier to bring your full self into rooms in which you have been denied entry or told to leave aspects of yourself behind in order to gain access when you know who you are and love who you are, even with all of your best assets and flaws. Now is the time to fully embrace ourselves in every aspect of our being in order to be ready for and push for the massive changes afoot throughout the industry in response to #BlackLivesMatter, #MeToo, #TimesUp, and the converging pandemics of COVID-19 and racial injustice. Equipped with the ability to break down the audition process rather than being broken down by its toxicity, we hope you will find not only success as an actor, but also a journey of self-love and self-discovery that amplifies your work as an actor and your voice as a human being.

I

ESTABLISHING AND BREAKING BOUNDARIES

Centering Wellness

Boundaries and wellness can revolutionize your audition practice and enhance your ability to land roles. *Boundary* is just another word for a limit. Establishing boundaries is part of your self-care as an actor. Identifying them, setting them, maintaining them, and breaking them are all part of your personal and professional development. Sometimes we have no idea when a boundary has been crossed until it has actually happened, or that we even need to set boundaries in order to maintain safe working practices. Everyone needs limits to maintain safety and security for our individual and collective well-being.

The entertainment industry establishes its own boundaries that can dictate or limit access to roles or opportunities for artists by raising questions like: What "type" are you? What roles will you play? Are you better at comedy or drama? Are you under- or overweight? Are your hair texture and color or skin color "just right"? These troubling aspects of the entertainment industry and casting process make this business very intellectually challenging most of the time, leaving many actors, particularly actors of the global majority, feeling powerless, especially when trying to book jobs through auditions.

As an actor, you have the greatest control of your perspective and can use your self-knowledge and discovery to your advantage in spite of the limitations of the industry. If you believe everything a director says about you, you will be changing yourself every week. If you let racial, ethnic, gender, ability, class, and sexual identification stereotypes define who you are, you will be miserable. Again, this list includes a variety of characteristics for which an actor might experience discrimination, but the following discussion is specifically about dealing with stereotypes as an actor of the global majority.

As the #BlackLivesMatter and #MeToo movements have revealed, the industry needs a lot of work. Throughout this book, we encourage you to see these challenges for what they are and prepare yourself for them by setting boundaries that will help you offer your best performance in your auditions. Taking all of these factors into consideration during preparation and then throwing them out the door in performance will enable you to focus on how you approach the work with each opportunity. When you know who you are and what you stand for, no one can define that for you.

Many White-identifying actors, casting directors, and directors may try to tell you that you are "making too big a deal" about race, sexuality, gender, ability, class, and other stereotypes. However, they rarely, if ever, have to worry about their work experiences departing from non-White experiences. At times, White actors and directors may be called on to portray non-White characters and experiences, which can lead to another set of issues, considering the previously discussed racial disparities in casting and directing opportunities. On the flip side, actors of the global majority working in the United States rarely, if ever, have the daily luxury of auditioning for a part that was written by someone of their same racial identity, ethnicity, class position, cultural experiences, and so on. In fact, most actors of the global majority who have the opportunity of working are performing in roles that are predominantly written by White writers. Some White writers write transracially in convincing ways that are inspiring to artists of the global majority. Others traffic in aspirational or fantastical ideas about people of color based on thinly imagined or lived interactions.

Many casting directors must rely on scripts and casting breakdowns that may offer superficial representations of identity in order to cast parts. Remember that the casting directors did not write the scripts. Many casting directors are good at casting, but may lack the cultural literacy and fluency to discuss the reasons why characters are written as they are on the page. Many casting directors engage in microaggressive behavior with actors by asking them to perform racial, ethnic, gender, or sexuality stereotypes because they lack critical fluencies in appropriate discourse of race, ethnicity, gender, and sexuality that are grounded in intersectionality.

Intersectionality is an identity theory developed by critical race theorist Kimberlé Crenshaw and expounded on by Black feminist theorist Patricia Hill Collins that suggests that race, ethnicity, class, gender, sexuality, and ability are overlapping aspects of identity that cannot be isolated just because someone asks us to self-present using one facet of our identity.[1] Unless you work with artists who are culturally literate and inclusive of the work and experiences of people of the global majority—whether written and played, directed, and produced by those representing the range and depth of their respective cultural backgrounds—you can guarantee that you will run into stereotypes on the job. Recognizing that cultural literacy and fluency are lacking in many positions of power, and there is no excuse for it, part of your job as a professional in a historically inequitable industry is to anticipate stereotypes in the writing, in the room, and throughout the industry at large.

In any scenario, it is up to actors to be prepared and to know our personal limits before we show up in the room to audition for the job. Asking many questions about yourself, what you want as a professional, and what the character in the script wants can help you align your talents and technical ability with the needs of the character. But first, let us talk a bit more about how to establish boundaries.

HOW TO ESTABLISH BOUNDARIES

As an actor you need to know your limits and be honest with yourself about what you can do in terms of skill and what you are willing to do in terms of values. Knowing your limits before you engage with casting directors can help you navigate the process. Casting directors are human resource professionals for the theater, film, and television industries. They match hundreds of actors daily as potential candidates for parts. Because casting directors have so much experience, they will quickly pick up on a lie, so don't lie on your résumé about something you can't really do. It doesn't pay off in the long run.

Hopefully, you are always striving to increase your skillsets and to grow as an artist. It is counterproductive to go into an audition that requires a skillset you truly do not have, especially if you are unwilling to prepare in advance. Casting directors will know when you're fudging your way through a skillset and wasting your time and theirs.

In addition to being truthful with the casting director about the skills you can bring to a part, you need to be clear about what types of roles you are willing to perform and what activities you are willing to engage in during auditions. For example, are you comfortable with extreme violence? Nudity? Animals on set? These decisions are very personal and very necessary. You are the only one who knows your moral compass and how it intersects or collides with your professional goals. When you clearly identify what you will and won't do before you agree to attend the audition, you can focus your energy on the opportunities that align with your personal and professional goals.

EXPECTING PROFESSIONALISM AND PROTECTION DURING AUDITIONS . . . OR THE LACK THEREOF

You should treat auditioning as a business practice. When you go on a job interview at any business, you expect professional environments and behaviors. You deserve to audition in a safe, respectable place of business during normal business hours. If you are asked to audition outside of business hours, please ask your representation why, and if there will be someone on site to protect talent. The #MeToo, #TimesUp, and #BlackLivesMatter movements have drawn attention to some of the inappropriate interactions taking place in the audition process and throughout the industry. As a result, there may be more oversight now than ever before in terms of how auditions are conducted.

Protecting your body is an important boundary. Don't do anything in an audition that is not professional, even if you are asked. There are certain protections union actors receive that non-union actors do not. Be clear on your status with the union, your representation, and yourself before you enter into more challenging physical material in your audition process. If you are agreeing to audition for a film with sexual or violent content, you should ask up front if there is required nudity or intimacy expected in the audition process. You should also inquire about the presence of an intimacy coach to consult on dealing with sex and violence. Similar dangers come into play with extreme physical comedy, stunts, and acrobatics. You should not be asked to do anything that is illegal, violent, invasive, dangerous, or salacious. If you are asked to do such things in an audition, please leave immediately and report the incident to your agent and the authorities.

Let's explore a few types of boundaries and how you establish them while becoming a stronger actor and human being.

Self

It is up to you to radically prioritize yourself and your world. You can decide what type of artist you want to be. You can create your own roadmap to achieve your dream. There is no magic unicorn fairy that comes to your door with your dream in a cute bag wrapped in tissue paper. You have to plan, work, edit, and repeat for as long as it takes to reach your goals. When you hit the goals that you desire, revise as needed and repeat until your career aligns with the goals you envision for yourself.

Teachers

Teachers in private lessons, studios, universities, or colleges should have safe boundaries established in their classrooms because it can be awkward for students to find security within those spaces. You do not have to accept any type of physical engagement from your teacher unless it is expressly engaged with the lesson and with your permission. When working in scenes, you should ask and give permission for any type of physical touch. Acceptable physical touch is limited to physical exercises that are part of the acting class, and even then should occur only with permission. Be specific and clear about boundaries with your teacher and fellow actors.

Self-Care

Identifying "safe words" in your acting process is important specifically when dealing with a scene that involves physical and emotional intimacy. Safe words can help you—whether in class or working on a job—to stop the action when you feel discomfort with the direction or the actions of a scene partner. You never know when you may experience triggers in class or on set that may disrupt your plan for the scene. Asking for a moment of self-care and/or understanding of your emotional and physical triggers as an actor before you work will allow you to create a safe space for yourself in your acting process.

Gestures, words, and directives that make studio art spaces seem "family like" are not necessarily so and should be met with caution. For example, when teachers or directors say things like "we're family" or "this is a team" or "what happens here stays here," make sure that you understand that these statements must be taken in the context of a business environment. Having a "work team" or a "work family" is very different than an actual family. Teachers or entertainment professionals offering you massages because "you look tense," or asking students to disrobe for "more freedom," are highly problematic requests that should be considered unprofessional. You have the right to reject these advances and to also ask to be excused from any classroom or studio environment where unwanted touching or suggestion takes place.

Sometimes teachers in studio dance or voice class will ask to put their hand on your diaphragm or adjust an arm or leg in a posture. You have the power to grant or refuse permission and let your teachers know where and when they can touch your body. This is also true for verbal engagement. Many acting, dance, and voice teachers in- and outside of the university environment use harsh language or so-called "real" language to talk to actors. Using profanity, demeaning comments, or unflattering comparisons is another form of hazing and should be avoided at all times. You deserve to be seen and heard in your learning and rehearsal spaces. When you start to feel unsafe, sad, or disconnected, these emotions may be signs that you need to readjust where you are in the room and make a safe space for yourself.

Boundaries with Casting Directors, Directors, Professors, Agents, and Others

The #MeToo and #TimesUp movements have further exposed long-standing challenges in the entertainment industry. Female, male, and nonbinary actors have been manipulated by those who have power and control over actors' job opportunities and work lives. We implore you to stand up for yourself and others. If you see something that is equivalent to verbal, psychological, sexual, or physical assault, or if any person in an authority position uses their power and position to make you feel cornered or frightened, report it. You have the right to file a claim with human resources, campus Office of Institutional Opportunity and Access (IOA), the police (city or campus), or any other authorities in your city, studio, or campus. In the event that you or someone you know is physically assaulted, please contact the police immediately and file a claim. Engaging professionals to help you navigate difficult and dangerous practices is key. You are not to blame for another person's inappropriate behavior. Contrary to popular lore, you do not have to compromise your physical or emotional safety to advance your career. You have the authority to say "no" to any job or acting experience that makes you feel unsafe at any time. Your career will advance when you are safe and secure.

If you experience verbal or sexual assault of any kind, report it to an authority immediately. Overall, the aforementioned boundaries are suggestions for actors to develop action steps that they can use to evaluate and create safe working environments.

Boundaries about the Truth—Honesty Is Key

Rejection is a constant in this industry, even for the most famous and critically acclaimed actors. So, if you're going to pursue acting, you should be very clear about why you want to be an actor. Many acting teachers will tell you that if you don't *need* to act, you should do something else. There are working actors who are not famous or rich but are able to make a living acting. There are countless others who work multiple jobs while pursuing acting. It is not an easy field to break into, so in order to stay on track, it's important to have a mission statement. This mission statement will verbalize what you hope to accomplish by pursuing a career in acting.

For example, some people enter the profession because they want to be seen and expect to become rich and famous. They are most interested in playing themselves or being personalities as opposed to working a craft or playing a range of characters. Others enter the profession because they identify as artists, motivated by the need to tell stories by working their craft. We are not proposing one or the other, but you should be honest with yourself about why you are entering the profession.

Understanding your motivations for pursuing acting will help you determine how to select roles. If you have decided to pursue acting as a personality, you will seek only those roles that align with your personality, look, target audience, and interests. There are certain workshops, seminars, and training that can help you better capitalize on your brand as a personality. For example, auditioning to be a personality on a reality show is very different from auditioning for a role on a sitcom or drama series. In terms of auditioning, you would only pursue opportunities that align with this, and although you may be considered for alternative roles, your guidelines will help you determine whether they are of interest to you.

Whether or not you have an agent, you should be proactive in your search for opportunities and be prepared to advocate on your own behalf as needed. Actors without agents have to advocate for themselves regardless, but those with representation may also have greater support (although some agents are more interested in your booking than your rights). If you have an agent, be sure to share your boundaries and make clear how you understand your working relationship to secure your employment. You should learn as much as you can about what protections exist for you and how to access them should you need them.

The same expectations that you have for respect and dignity in the work that you do at any other type of job are what you should demand and expect when working as an actor. Simple questions about pay rate, time worked, treatment of employees, and so on are important fundamental questions. If you are a member of an actor's union, it is your responsibility to learn the union rules and regulations so that you understand when you or your employer are out of compliance. As an actor of the global majority, if you have heard from fellow actors that a certain director exhibits racist behavior when working, take such a claim seriously and attempt to verify the account. Ultimately, we cannot make decisions on hearsay, but when you receive information, you can avoid acting on or reproducing false claims against actors, directors, and casting directors by following your personal channels of verification and making sure that you follow professional protocols and report behavior that is unprofessional. With such important information, you can use your best judgment to make an informed decision about whether or not

you are willing to consent to work in a potentially racist environment and determine how you will navigate it should you choose to
proceed. If you knew that the CEO of a certain company had political beliefs that did not align with your moral code of ethics, you
might not apply for a job at that company. Similarly, you can save
yourself time and energy by turning down an audition that could
place you in a racist environment and letting your agent or manager
know that you are passing based on personal conflicts.

Without judgment, we encourage you to know where you stand
as an artist. These guidelines can help you simplify your process as
an actor and make informed, educated decisions about the work you
do and where you do it.

BOUNDARIES BEFORE AND DURING THE AUDITION

Before you audition, you should consider the type of career you
hope to have and the types of roles it will take to achieve it. You
might consider the actors you admire and what types of roles they
have played. You should also keep in mind whether these actors
represent the same types of characters you might be considered to
play now or at other stages of your career. Mapping out a career
trajectory based on the careers of actors you admire can be a helpful
strategy, one that can and should be adapted with new discoveries.
Know in advance what types of roles you are willing or unwilling to
play. Be honest about what you are willing or unwilling to do in
terms of the types of roles and auditioning process. If the role requires nudity, you should know before you go to the audition if you
are willing to do such a role and speak with your agent, if you have
one, about how this will be handled in the audition and production
process should you be cast. If you are treated poorly or discriminat-
ed against while auditioning, please report the incident to your rep-
resentative.

Likewise, if the role traffics in racist, sexist, gendered, or ageist
stereotypes, you should have guidelines that help you determine if
this is a role or project you will pursue. Communicate with your

agent about these guidelines in advance so that you don't waste your time or anyone else's on a project that does not align with your personal or professional goals. Here is an example of a fictional breakdown for a casting for an independent film. There is important information included about each character that can help you get a feel for the part before you even get the script.

CASTING BREAKDOWN

Thursday, Aug. 27, 2021, 6:15 AM CENTRAL

THE BUBBLE

First of a series revolving around these characters

> Union Status: NON-UNION
> Producer: Janice Doe
> Writer/Director: John Doe
> Director of Photography: Anyman Jones
> Casting Director: Delia Doe
> Audition: Casting from reels and Eco cast self-tapes
> Start Date: 10/02/2021, 10/03/2021, 10/04/2021
> Rate: Unpaid
> Location: DETROIT, MI

SUBMISSION DEADLINE: 09/12/2021

PLEASE INCLUDE SIZE CARDS. IF POSSIBLE, PLEASE SUBMIT ACTOR'S ONLINE DEMO CLIPS ALONG WITH EACH ACTOR SUBMISSION.

THE BUBBLE is a new streaming series created by Jane Doe on Netflix involving a tech start-up in Detroit on the rise. These twenty- and thirty-somethings are doing everything they can to make it to the top to become the next Instagram, but at what cost? Seeking series regulars and supporting cast members. All ethnicities encouraged.

[TRAY]

Twenty-five to thirty years old, AFRICAN AMERICAN. Hip-hop style, but clean-shaven. Hitman that works with Hershel. He is fit and woke with lots of swagger. He is determined to prove himself at his job and to his partner Hershel. He's an attorney for the tech firm. LEAD

- *Break It Down note*: Look for clues here—"hip-hop style" and "swagger" are clues of stereotyping that may indicate they want the Black actor to be the "hip" one in the cast. Think about this as you read the other character breakdowns below.

[HERSHEL]
Twenty-five to thirty-five years old, male. LATINO. Very J. Crew/Brooks Brothers appearance. Executive type with a chip on his shoulder. Speaks Spanish. Wants to help his boy Tray, but not at his own expense. He has a lot on the line, and he must make partner in this firm first. LEAD

- *Break It Down note*: Clues here are "Latino," "speaks Spanish," which is information offered with no story context, and "help his boy," which lets you know he may be "down" with Tray and that the producers may ask the actor to speak Spanish at some point in the audition to prove that he can. Think about the relationship between the two characters if you get sides (remember: sides are segments of the script issued to actors for auditions) between Hershel and Tray.

[DEONDRA]
Twenty-six to thirty years old, female. BLACK OR LATINA. Tall and very sexy. Model look. Wears revealing clothing to work to get ahead. Down to earth with a little stripper vibe. Trying to escape an abusive boyfriend relationship when she stumbles upon the partners and finds a great job and maybe a new fling along the way. SUPPORTING

- *Break It Down note*: The racial play between Black or Latina lets you know that the casting here is arbitrary and that the writers just want a woman of color in the office. The racial identity of the character may or may not have anything to do with the story line. The writers have sexualized the role as sexually provocative ["stripper vibe"] and have no real substance for the character's needs or wants in the breakdown. Think about who this character is supporting in the scene where your character reads with any of the leads. Mind the power dynamic.

[RILEY]
Twenty-two to twenty-seven ASIAN. Smart, funny, and rich tech guy. Think Yang. Kind of nerdy but very physically fit. Learns from the firm's partners how to be a real lady's man. Has everything but the hot girl. SUPPORTING

- *Break It Down note:* Asian American stereotypes abound here. Smart, tech geek, and so on, all Asian and Asian American stereotypical traits of the model minority. As an Asian or Asian American actor, seeing these descriptions gives you a heads up about the aesthetic ideas of the writers. You will have to decide how or if you want to play a role like this. The idea of learning how to be a "ladies' man" is sexist and infantilizing here. This breakdown suggests you may be disappointed by the script, given the prevalence of stereotypes.

We hope that reviewing these types of breakdowns won't make you upset, but rather more prepared for how completely ridiculous some of these casting briefs can be. Once you can read these descriptors and decide what works for you and what you want, you can approach these microaggressive descriptions with a strategy that may empower you to make choices in the room that subvert the narrow-minded ideas you see or play into them in ways that you are comfortable with as an actor. We want you to see the connection between the breakdown information that you receive, the script, and the expectations of the casting directors and directors. Sometimes what they want is clear, and sometimes it is completely convoluted.

Don't take any of it personally. It is business, although it can be harmful. Some parts of the business are carried out in a really racist way; other parts have more inclusive behavior and you will find people challenge breakdowns that socially and culturally demean talent. But the sad part is that sometimes people of the global majority in the industry write breakdowns like the ones you see above because that has been the standard practice that has been taught and deployed as the norm. If you come across such breakdowns, be prepared to set your boundaries, ask informed questions, and make assessments about the whole project in relationship to the character you are called to audition for. Always remember you can decline the part later if you're not happy with the answers to your questions.

BREAKING IT DOWN—ESTABLISH YOUR LIMITS

There are so many industry and societal obstacles stacked up against actors of the global majority as a result of systemic racism in the business that there does come a point where you have to turn your attention toward yourself. It is part of your professional responsibility as an actor to have your personal life worked out before you get to the audition. The first step is to be proud of your racial, ethnic, gender, sexual, and class identities and ability as parts of a simultaneous human existence, not a character description used by casting directors. Starting on this path of self-care can help you affirm the existence and the career paths you have established for yourself.

At the end of each chapter, we will provide you with a series of exercises or reflections to help you advance in your goals as an actor. We encourage you to write these reflections in a special journal—perhaps a beautiful blank book, or just a computer document that you devote to this project.

1. Write down the roles that you hope to play that would make you the proudest of yourself and that align with your personal values and worldviews.
2. Write down the roles that would undermine your values/goals as an artist.
3. Write down your three biggest fears and how they impact your work.
4. Write down three action steps you can make to address your fears.

5. Write down your top three qualities. How can you use these qualities in your work?

6. Ask yourself if there is anything that can be done in performance that aligns with your mission and moral compass. When you get an audition, ask yourself if this is the type of material you want to put into the world.

7. List actors you admire (your type or otherwise), and track the types of roles they played that align with your mission.

8. List specific examples of roles you would be willing or unwilling to play. Keep that list close to you as you make decisions.

9. Write your mission statements asserting your purpose as a human being on the planet and your purpose as an artist in the field.

10. Outline a wellness plan for what you will do before, during, and after an audition to ensure your well-being and sense of wholeness.

Be honest with yourself about why you're doing this thing called acting. Learn as much as you can about the industry so that you understand how to keep yourself healthy and safe. Write down your personal mission statement and know that you are not less of an artist if you refuse roles that do not align with your mission. Establish clear guidelines for yourself, and make decisions based on those guidelines, not the opinions of others; you have to live with you. Whatever you decide, commit to yourself first, and then move forth to craft the best performance you can so that you can audition on your terms.

2

TELL THE TRUTH

Telling the truth is a lifelong process, not a destination. Truth-telling is not as easy as it sounds. As you change over time, your truth changes. Depending on where you are in your career—beginning, middle, long, glorious end—not addressing this step can stand between you and every audition you take to book a job.

You have two places to focus: your personal truth and the truth of the character you are playing. To tell the truth, without any pretense, you have to decide what you want. Why do you want to be an actor? Do you want fame? Do you want to prove someone wrong? Do you want to be right? Do you want to be loved for your work? The entanglement of our truth, or lack thereof, with our career goals is complex.

Our advice is to figure out your current answers to these types of questions before you decide to take a job as an actor. Working as an actor is a different experience from working at Google, Starbucks, or any number of jobs that don't require you to perform texts before an audience that may trigger emotional and visceral responses. This is not to say that emotional and physical responses to interaction do not come into play in these types of non-acting jobs. However, actors engage with material intended to evoke emotional responses in audiences and due to the nature of the job may encounter the emotions themselves in the process.

As an actor, you have to identify actions that can help you summon emotion on demand. If you consent to play a role as a woman who has suffered verbal abuse, you have no idea how you may be triggered by that text on the job. A response that is yours as the actor and not that of the character you are portraying can easily result in redirection from the director or even firing. If you have an emotional response on your non-acting job, you can excuse yourself and return after you compose yourself. On a stage, film, or television set, there are only so many times you can take a time-out to get yourself together before you are replaced. If you are walking into an audition in an effort to fix personal problems, pay bills, or make people love you, you will not do well. Your desire to be an actor has to be bigger than your problems, ego, or sense of being right. Due to the competitive nature of the business, it is vital to truly want to do this work because many actors struggle for a long time.

If you are an actor of the global majority, your acting journey is even more challenging because you have to face the many stereotypes and microaggressions that are produced by the systemic racism in the entertainment business. As actors of the global majority attempt to reconcile their relationship to White supremacy, anti-Blackness, and other verbal violence, aggressions, and misrepresentations, you also have to learn your sides (*sides* is industry speak for segments of the script issued by casting directors, artistic directors, or directors that actors read from to audition) and present yourself as confidently as possible in the audition room. To get to your truth is a journey that is better done with a therapist and a wellness plan in advance rather than with an acting partner during an audition. We highly recommend that you identify someone, professional or personal, with whom you can share your hopes and fears, traumas and triumphs, in a safe, encouraging, and productive environment.

We encourage you to get in touch with your personal truth as an actor as you separate yourself from personal obstacles in a script. Knowing your truth and what you will stand for and what you won't can build your confidence before you walk into the room. As you enter the room as your full self, leave your baggage at the door or surrender it to someone who can help you sort out what you need and what you don't. Knowing that you are enough before you walk into the room to get the job is half the audition battle. Knowing that you will not get in your own way gives you a competitive edge that will signal to casting directors and directors that not only do you know your craft or your brand, but you also know who you are and feel good in your skin.

LET'S START WITH PERSONAL TRUTH

Who you are is all you have. What does this mean? It means that you are an amalgamation of everything good, bad, and indifferent that has ever happened to you. Your emotional DNA, experiences, and culture are wells you can draw from to prepare for your audition, rather than expendable material to be discarded due to shame or uncertainty.

Acting is one of only a few professions that asks you to constantly deal with your personal life experiences, emotions, and traumas. Many casting directors, directors, and acting teachers may not agree with this idea. Many acting professionals or teachers may say that all you have to do is say the lines written by the playwright or screenwriter; some others might say you have to "become" the character, while others suggest that your personal life and the character's life have nothing to do with one another and the rest will come. No matter what your opinion, one fact remains: you are the performer playing the emotional, social, and physical circumstances of the character. With this in mind, you have to consider the emotional impact and toll on your mind, body, and spirit when you play roles that may trigger your life experiences in some way.

Acting teachers are not therapists, nor are casting directors and directors. However, these various occupations do hold power. You are surrendering your emotional and physical safety to a director once you book a job. The more in tune you are with yourself and what feels right and safe for you, the more prepared you will be to accept or reject parts that may place you in a vulnerable space that does not feel comfortable or help you achieve the most productive performance. Be professional. Know your limits. No job is worth you feeling as if you have let yourself down because you crossed a personal boundary.

Black and non-Black actors of the global majority do the majority of their acting from scripts that are not written by people who look or sound like them. What happens when you have to play a character who is written as supposedly "Black," "Asian," "Native American," or "Hispanic," yet nothing they say or do resonates with the experiences of people of the global majority in the social and cultural contexts that the writer documents on the page? Our reactions to bad writing and stereotyping of people of color happen in the audition process, and the impact varies. We hear the words coming out of our mouths, but we often cannot reconcile the actions of the characters because they feel fake to us. When your acting does not align with stereotypical expectations, it may limit your ability to book the job, or it can open new avenues for considering the characterization, assuming the performance is rooted in the character as written on the page, even as it departs from the stereotype.

Overtly negative reactions to the stereotype while in the room may also affect booking potential but may be necessary if it does not align with your goals and purpose. This is why it is helpful to know as much as you can about the role and creative team in advance and decide whether or not you are willing to take such a role. In short, productive adaptation of a problematic stereotype could work for or against your ability to book the job. Reconciling the quality of our work with the quality of the texts we play is a lifelong journey. Performing according to your truth and the truth of the character beyond the stereotype is the key.

Though this book is not about personal therapy, we do recommend that you seek professional assistance and opportunities to discuss experiences that may block you from performing difficult texts. By *difficult texts*, we mean those that contain the following challenges, which may trigger emotional and unreconciled responses from actors of the global majority:

1. Playing White characters (when you are not White). This can be extremely difficult, particularly when casting directors and directors present you the role as a "gift" or "challenge" that is important for you because you are an "actor of color" or that somehow by erasing your racial identity or ethnicity you are proving you can act. These are microaggressions that fuel the racial, ethnic, and cultural omissions that occur when you are forced to pretend that your body's history does not come to bear on the text you play. Race does matter. History matters. Culture is a deep well that can source performance in any role.

2. Stereotypes. Specific triggers might occur when you are asked to "act" or "talk" more like your racial or ethnic identity, as if that were even possible. Questions such as "Can you act a little more Black? More Asian? More Latinx?" are basically offensive directives that presuppose a way of being and becoming that is based on dominant mythologies of race.

3. Dialogue. Some texts contain dialogue that is written to sound generically non-White. In some cases, this vernacular is written as "urban," with little racial or ethnic specificity in the written historical context. This can also work in reverse, when actors of the global majority are assumed to be unable to speak in prose or verse with heightened texts simply because they are not White. Likewise, we want to underline the assumption that AGM have fluency in vernacular language usage, which may not be the case.

All of these incidents can produce emotional triggers that make it difficult for actors to do their jobs, specifically because they are tied to attributes and qualities that have nothing to do with an actor's talent or technique. Recognizing the historical risk in doing so, we recommend thinking critically about work that you choose to audition for in the entertainment industry and be prepared to stand up for yourself as needed. Weigh the risks in relation to your values and know that you do have greater choices than those who have come before you, although the industry may tell you that you do not. The industry patterns will tell you that actors of color have to take what they can get in the entertainment industry because you have to "pay your dues." We don't believe that any actor should have to "pay dues" by playing roles that seek to demean underrepresented communities directly or indirectly due to poor writing or performative representation. The industry can and should do better, and there are artists who can value you and your work even if they have limited access to resources.

Acting is therapeutic, but it is not therapy and, in our view, should not be used as a surrogate for counseling, and doing so in the audition process could be disastrous. You have the right to accept whatever jobs you choose without explaining or defining your choices to cultural insiders or community members. You are a free agent. Your body will sometimes represent your entire community. With that said, stand strong in who you are and what you believe, and leave your personal drama at the door or, better yet, at home as you bring your full self into the audition room and the role if you book it.

If you read a script and it does not align with your views or skillsets, you're better off passing than going to the audition to prove a point to yourself or to someone else. The legacy you build as an artist begins as soon as you accept work. What you leave behind is up to you.

Acting truthfully in imaginary circumstances is the job of the actor, but how exactly do you do that? It starts with you and continues with the character you are called on to portray. Your race, ethnicity, gender, class, levels of mobility, and sexuality are facets of your identity that you cannot erase, hide, or silence when you enter a room, nor should you separate the qualities of who you are. The more confident you can become about yourself, the better you will feel about who you are as you lend your body and voice to play another character. Knowing where you begin and end in relation to the character is a profoundly helpful place to start.

Acting in the moments, the given circumstances, provided by the writer is your job as an actor. The given circumstances concern where you are and what you are doing as the character. Before you make up a backstory or imagine yourself as the character, you have to find the truth that the character is experiencing in the story as it is written. Look for clues in the narrative of the script that you can play in the room. Where is the character and why? How is the character feeling? How do they respond to other characters? How do they hear what another character is saying to them? What time of day is it? What state of mind is the character in during the moment of your sides? These are key questions to consider.

When writers write people of the global majority, the narrative of the text can shift depending on who is writing the story and their familiarity with the culture being represented. Plays, television, and film scripts that traffic in racial, ethnic, gender, class, and sexual identity stereotypes may be triggering to artists of the global majority. Regardless of who is writing the script, stereotypes can arise due to the historical patterns and pressures throughout the industry. The more in tune you are with yourself, the more you can ground yourself in your truth so that when these stereotypes show up in scripts, you are prepared to play the character with gravitas or turn down the role. The last thing you want is to be caught off guard by stereotyping during an audition, as the impact on your performance and psyche can be harmful.

White actors auditioning for White characters that remain unmarked as "raced" in scripts may have a different experience from actors of the global majority. Such characters are rarely described as White unless there is an ethnic specificity to their Whiteness that is integral to the character's life (i.e., the character is Italian or German American and that ethnic identity shapes the story). A White actor may bring this particularity into an audition and experience certain stereotyping associated with these groups but without the same pressures as actors of the global majority who cannot pass as White. In such cases, the White actor's Whiteness expands the possibilities of perceived individuality and flexibility to play other White characters beyond the specified group.

When characters are specifically written as historically underrepresented communities, no matter what the period, an individual character's experience is often used to represent the whole of a particular group. For example, in the movie *The Help* (2011), a period piece based on a book by a White writer, Viola Davis plays a Black maid working in the early 1960s. Many people consider the representation of a Black maid as a negative depiction of African Americans. But Viola Davis and Octavia Spencer (who also plays a maid in the movie) subvert the notion of maids as Black stereotypes through performance. They took the opportunity to honor the African American women who served as maids in real life.

How did they do this? They did not judge the roles. They did not use a twenty-first-century understanding of race to play parts that took place in the mid-twentieth century. They mined the sociohistorical circumstances by understanding the hierarchical relationships between White women and their Black maids. They found subversive moments within the limitations of the script. Both actresses used subversive looks and gestures. They found ways to connect emotion with the action in the lines that let the audience know that though they were in "subservient roles," the characters they played had some agency and influence within the homes where they were employed. Although Davis later expressed regret for her role in the film, her nuanced portrayal is still a notable example of the skill required to humanize potentially stereotypical representations in performance.

Black actresses of the twentieth century—such as Hattie McDaniel, who played a maid in *Gone with the Wind*—played the only roles available for Black women at the time. Even though McDaniel's performance made her the first African American to win an Oscar, for Best Supporting Actress, she and many other African American actresses in Hollywood had to face the fact that the entertainment industry is invested in stereotypical representations because they often make money. *Gone with the Wind* was and is one of the most successful films in Hollywood history. Since its debut in 1939, the film has grossed over 390 million dollars.[1] Many actors of the global majority, from Halle Berry to Sophia Vergara, have played stereotypes for tremendous financial gain. Is Hollywood's investment in stereotypes of all kinds good? No. Is this racist? Yes, in many instances. Are stereotypes a reality of this business? Again, yes. Actors of the global majority must decide who we are in relationship to, or distinctly different from, the types of roles that we *choose* to play.

In the twenty-first century, there is an idea in entertainment that actors are somehow lucky to have an agent or manager representation. Yet little attention is paid to the institutional inequality embedded in the entertainment industry and the disproportionate ways that performers of the global majority are represented, paid, and treated. However, our relationships with agents, managers, and casting directors are business relationships. We should be interviewing our representatives in the same way that they interview us for representation. Our agent representatives should be culturally literate advocates for us. If you are asked to play a part that you feel is demeaning to you or that triggers you in some personal way, you can decline the audition completely as a *business* decision that is in the best interest of your self-care and professional brand. The more we can distinguish our sense of self and well-being from the roles we choose to play, the healthier our relationship with our acting career will be.

Auditions are job interviews, so read the descriptions carefully before you apply. Ask important questions of your representatives before you agree to audition for a job. If the script seems racist, sexist, homophobic, ableist, and so on, the project very well could be.

NOW, THE TRUTH ABOUT THE CHARACTER

You have to find and tell the truth about what's on the page when you perform in the audition room. In order to find the truth about what's on the page, you have to get the sides as far in advance as possible, preferably before you get to the audition. In this instance, use it to your advantage: study the information you are given, and fill in any gaps by conducting research. Remember, however, that your research must be guided by what's on the page.

Typically, the agent and casting director breakdown (the brief description of the character's personality, look, and role in the story used to identify potential actors for the role) will provide information about the character, setting, time period, and scene context. Make sure you understand all of the words and are able to pronounce them as the character. If you are unclear about meaning or pronunciation, look it up. You should not discover at the audition that you do not know what a word means or how to say it. Work with what is there on the page.

Let's take a look at a fictional breakdown for a film:

PIPELINE PRODUCTIONS (fictional breakdown)
FEBRUARY 20, 2020
"PICKING UP THE PIECES"
NETWORK: Showtime—one-hour Dramedy
DIRECTOR: JAMES DOE
CASTING DIRECTOR: JULIE UPFORIT

This is a pilot for a "Girlfriends meets Girls"–style show from showrunner Ava Duvernay. PICKING UP THE PIECES is a thirty-something hour dramedy about a group of artist friends who are late in career and have not quite made it in their respective careers. The show pivots from the idea that it's either now or never. The friends are on a fast and furious run toward their goals before time runs out and they turn forty.

DEJA (36)—Afro-Latinx, really good looking "for her age." Former kid star turned personal assistant. Feisty, with a temper. Looking for a break before it's too late.

PAULA (35)—single, divorced mother of one. Lives in a vegan communal home with other single, upwardly mobile mothers.

LEA (33)—African American, non-binary. Ceramicist trying to make it in the fine arts scene but is now selling her work on Etsy. She's a social media darling, but the focus is on her quirky ceramics, not her, which is a bummer.

RON (32)—Mixed-identified Black-Asian male. Model and social media influencer. Working to get his last men's wear show
in Paris. In an on-again, off-again relationship with Lea.

DUKE (34)—Korean American, fitness trainer. Working to get a
fitness channel show for years to no avail. The pressure from his
perfect siblings to get his perfect life together builds as he man-
ages competition from younger, hotter trainers.

Many actors have the idea that they "create the character," but
this could not be further from the truth. Take a look at the fictional
characters above. There is not much "depth" for any actor to go on
to prepare an audition; however, there are clues in this breakdown
that can help the actor identify the style and tone of the new series.
The first clue is that it is a pilot. A pilot is a show "audition" for
networks that helps them decide if they want to invest in future
episodes. When you audition for a pilot, you have the potential to
originate the character, which means if you book it, you will be the
first actor to play this character in a brand-new show.

The second clue is that this is an hour-long dramedy on Showtime. This should give you a bit of information about tone. Looking
for shows that have a blend of comedy and drama, thus *dramedy*, on
the network that fit this category will help you understand how to
interpret the style of the show when you get the script. The playwright or screenwriter writes the character as they imagine it in the
world of the play, television show, or film. Your job is to play what
is on the page as the character's story is revealed moment to moment in the script.

The third clue lies in the description of the characters. This show
appears to want a multiracial group of friends who all work in a job
that they are not yet successful in. The common theme is that they
want to "make it" before they are forty. If these characters seem
shallow from the breakdown, they probably are. Look at the script
sides, and make as many connections as you can.

Other clues that are obvious here are the racial and physical identifiers presented in the breakdown about the characters. This is a multiracial show, and the casting appears to be very purposeful. We used Ava DuVernay as a show creator because she is known for creating shows for actors of the global majority. The description of the show states *Girlfriends* (2000, created by Mara Brock Akil) meets *Girls* (2011, created by Lena Dunham). This is another important clue. Watch a few episodes of each show (both shows are now canceled but run "on demand" on Netflix and HBO, respectively). Taking notes about how the themes and acting styles may cross over, as described in the breakdown, may help you interpret tone and vibrancy of the characters a bit more.

Other key clues here that can help you map the breakdown are the names of the director, casting director, and network. Do your research and make sure that you have not only applied our steps but also taken the time to grab all of the information you can from the original breakdown about these players. See what type of talent the casting directors cast. Do they give breaks to new talent? Does the director have a great track record with pilots? The more you know, the more informed you are in your preparation.

The actor only has the luxury of knowing what happens in the entire story if they have the whole script. When you are auditioning, nine times out of ten, you won't have the entire play, film, or TV episode, so you have to play what is on your sides to the best of your ability. If the play you are auditioning for is previously published, you can and should buy a copy. Build your library of material as part of your professional development. If you are auditioning for a television show that has already aired, you can go back and watch previously taped episodes to determine the tone and vibrancy of the dialogue in the show. If you are auditioning for a film, look at the director's and writer's previous work to see if you can learn anything about the director's aesthetic and the writer's storytelling. For example, does the director ask the principal characters to make big choices? Does the director like very crisp dialogue delivery, or do you notice a more reality-based delivery where parts of the actors' lines are lost? If you are auditioning for a commercial for a well-known allergy medicine, for example, try to learn as much as you can about the previous campaign to discover the tone of the brand. Do your research.

You should also have some knowledge about the casting director you are auditioning for at all times. Do they give breaks to new talent? Do you notice any patterns in types or other details? Learning about the story and the tone and creative team enables you to tap into a world of the script and expectations for the role.

In order to prepare for an audition, we encourage you to take the time to do the research, or at least a quick Google search. Read a review or watch a quick glimpse on YouTube of the play, television show, or film style you're auditioning for. We also suggest that you read the trades and performance review sections of national newspapers such as the *New York Times* so that you can stay abreast of what is happening in the entertainment industry. If you were a stockbroker, you would read the business section of the newspaper and watch the stock market. We ask that, as an actor, you read the industry trades so that you will be informed about job opportunities and current trends. All of these steps can help build a strong foundation for an informed audition.

Truth is essential to the entire process of auditioning. While research can help you prepare for the audition, ultimately the only thing that matters is that you present the character in the life they are living on the page. You have to get truthful about your look, abilities, skills, and other characteristics. You waste time in the pursuit of becoming a working actor when you are in denial about who you are, what you are capable of doing, and what is on the page. Don't lie.

Make sure you pay attention to any details provided like age, race, ethnicity or nationality, time period, or circumstances; all of this will give you clues of the "truth" of the character according to the writer. The script (or sides) act as a guide for understanding what the general expectation of the character might be based on the information provided. If wardrobe details are provided, use them; even these and stage directions that suggest movement or shifts in tone are clues about what was expected by the writer, even though it may shift dramatically according to the vision of the director.

Be prepared to enact the director's vision when asked, but use the script or sides and the writer's insights as your anchor, the thing that you hold onto as needed to carry you through the audition. If you deviate from what is on the page, you decrease your likelihood of being cast. You are provided sides for a reason, so you should use them and become familiar with them. If you have time to do so, you should also memorize the lines, but keep your script in hand, which will free you to perform the character in the moment, again, according to the specifications of the script.

Generally, in an audition, you are there to test drive the role that was written as an interview to see how capable you are of doing the job. You are there to let the casting director know that you are capable of portraying the character that was written, first and foremost, and then you may be asked to demonstrate your ability to expand the role, but even in doing so, it must be based on what is actually there.

Should you be asked to improvise, it should still come from cues on the page. Don't invent a made-up sibling or some far-out deviation from the sociohistorical context of the play unless asked to do so, and even then, the text should be an anchor. The auditioners should be able to recognize the character and given circumstances even in an improvised performance. If not, there is no reason for you to be considered for this role.

There are some instances in which the director or casting directors are looking for deviations as part of the tone or process for the work (think something like Stew's *Passing Strange* [2008]). Again, always return to the page and be prepared to know everything you can about the character and their relationships based on reading everything in the sides, not just your part. At the time of the audition, the only thing that matters is that you present yourself truthfully as the character in the life they are living on the page. Again, you may feel inspired to try something different in the moment. This is a risk, and you have the power to choose whether or not to take it. Let the quest for truth be your guide and the page be your anchor. That way, if you decide to take off in a different direction, you have a compass to guide you back.

If you want to demonstrate range or creativity, you could experiment with deviating in a selected set of lines or actions while remaining true to the bulk of the material. But again, this is a risk and may be more of a distraction to the director and casting director than an asset to your audition. Advance preparation will help you determine if and how to take such a risk if the audition calls for it. Otherwise, just stick to the script and show the directors, first and foremost, how well you can execute the information provided; then you can show them how you would build on that. This is more often part of the callback process, but it sometimes happens at the first set of auditions, too, when a director instructs the actor to try something specific. So be open to experimentation and prepared for possible scenarios, but always draw from the script as your inspiration for everything you do in the audition.

TRUTH IS ESSENTIAL TO THE ENTIRE PROCESS OF AUDITIONING

If you can't convince the director or casting director, you will not have a chance to convince an audience. And when you think of convincing, think of it as storytelling—but telling a story that actually happens, even if it is fanciful and magical. This can only happen if you fully embrace the world the writer built and the director is envisioning, and you can only do that if you study the script and sides like your life depends on it. The life of your character actually does depend on it. Your character cannot live unless you breathe life into them. You are providing the breath for the body that the writer has sculpted. You will animate the body using your own body as an instrument to play each note the writer has written. You may offer a flourish for a particular note, but it still has to be the note that was written. You may extend or shorten it, even vary the key or tempo, but it has to be the same score. Otherwise, your version of the character may be too unrecognizable to even have a chance to enter the world the creative team is building to tell the story. Granted, sometimes they don't know exactly what they're looking for until they see it. But we have rarely seen an instance where someone deviates so far afield from the script that they become unrecognizable as the character and still get cast in that role.

HARD TRUTHS: GETTING REAL ABOUT YOUR LOOK, ABILITIES, AND SKILLS

You should be honest about your skills and abilities so you don't waste your time or the time of the people who are casting the roles. If you cannot sing or dance, you should not be auditioning for roles that specify these skills are needed for the character. Instead, you should train in these areas to develop the skills or stick to roles that do not require them. There are some instances in which people have these skills and are not aware of them, but that is precisely the point. If you are an actor, you should know your abilities, your strengths, and your areas that need development, so that you can use them to your advantage and develop them as needed.

In addition to your skills, your physical appearance will be heavily scrutinized and judged. Are you curvy? Muscular? Heavyset? According to whose standards? Is your nose too straight, wide, narrow? Is your hair too curly? Too straight? Too thin? Is your voice annoying? Too sexy? Too squeaky? These are hard truths to face, but you have to ask yourself, *Whose truths are these?* Casting directors, agents, teachers, managers, and a host of other people will try to tell you who you are. The media will present images of people who are supposedly "perfect." Again, you have to ask the question, *Perfect to whom?* The sooner you face your personal truth about who you are and what qualities you love (or hope to develop) about yourself, the easier it will be to focus on presenting yourself confidently in the audition room.

The entertainment industry is erroneously built on centering Eurocentric forms of beauty, so don't be caught off guard by snarky comments from potential employers. If you do not fit those so-called "norms," don't worry. Just affirm your beauty and sense of self, and know that no one can be you. No one can offer what you can offer. You are one of a kind. Own it. We can all get better, look better, feel better, according to our own standards. However, the sooner you accept your hard truths, the sooner you can identify your strengths and growth areas.

CONCLUSION

Not every role is for you, and that is also okay. There are fewer roles than there are actors, so rejection is a common occurrence even for the most sought-out actors. Don't waste your time beating yourself up about the roles you don't get. Instead, ask yourself, *Is there anything I can learn from how I tend to be cast or the types of roles I cannot grasp?*

Sometimes the answers are easy. Yes, the industry is racist, sexist, classist, ageist. These are facts. The more we understand the world we are entering, the more power we have to decide how we want to participate in it. If you are in your forties auditioning for roles of characters in their twenties, you need to stop. Find the roles that you are most likely to be cast in by being honest with yourself about how you look to others, how they might believably cast you, and what your skillsets are for playing any given role.

Beyond your skills and physical appearance, you can increase your chance of landing a role by paying close attention to subtle details in the script. If the script specifies that a particular song plays in the background or is sung by the character, be sure you know the song before you go to the audition. Such things are important clues about the time period, tone, culture, and so on, as well as an actor's commitment to preparation. In other words, so many clues about the performance the director is looking for are hidden in plain sight in the script or sides. To not use them basically tells your auditioners that you don't really want the role and are unwilling to prepare. You waste time in the pursuit of becoming a working actor when you are in denial about who you are, what you are capable of doing, and what is on the page. Don't lie. Discover and tell your truth.

TELL THE TRUTH—THREE REASONS JOURNAL PROMPTS

Please respond to these questions in your journal:

1. Name three things that excite you the most about being an actor.
2. Name three reasons why you want to be an actor.
3. How do your three reasons pertain to you achieving your goals as an actor?
4. Name three things that scare you about your past or present that can impact you achieving your goals in acting.
5. Identify three things that you have trouble accepting about yourself.
6. Name three things you can do to change the things listed above.
7. Identify three things that you love about yourself.
8. List three ways that you can use the things you like about yourself to help build your confidence in acting.

3

READ THE STORY, NOT THE LINES

Stories are part of our growth and development in every stage of life, especially as actors. As children we grow up listening to stories in various forms: reading aloud with parents, grandparents, and caregivers; listening to stories on television and in films; reading comic books; and enjoying video games, music, and dance. Humans need stories to survive and to cultivate hope. Enslaved Africans in the United States were forbidden to read by slave masters and state anti-literacy laws. Drawing on African cultural traditions, oral storytelling became the principal way for Black people, and other people of the global majority drawing from their traditions, to share stories about our cultures, our hopes, and our dreams. Stories are passed down from one generation to the next. We learn life lessons, history, skills, and more from stories.

Storytelling is the capacity to convincingly share the experiences of yourself, of others, or of imagination. Acting is simply playing your part convincingly in a story. In order to help people understand what your character needs, wants, and is doing in your scene, you have to also be aware of what everyone else is doing in the scene. The more you read the story, the more you can tell it. If I read *Goldilocks and the Little Bears* one time, I cannot really understand the needs of Goldilocks nor the feelings of the bears when they return to their home to find that their food has been eaten, beds slept in, and chairs broken.

Whatever part you are playing as an actor is connected to a larger story. Your job is to find all of the clues that you can within the script and to make as many connections as you can to tell the story in the most convincing way possible. You don't have to oversell or undersell. You don't have to yell, scream, or cry, unless you find your story requires it from what you unearth on the page.

Your imagination is important for your acting life. The text should ignite your imagination. You must read your script as many times as you possibly can so that you can understand where the story is coming from.

As discussed in chapter 2, if you can get access to the full script before the audition, you should. If your agent or manager cannot get you the script, do all you can to secure a copy. If the play, television show, or film is a new work and the script is not available, the sides are all you have, so they are the key to your performance.

When reading the story, be sure you have a general idea of the genre; not every story is intended to be realism. There are certain conventions associated with particular genres, so knowing if you are auditioning for something like *Get Out* (2017), which is a realism-based horror film, versus a skit for *Key and Peele* that requires comedic training and improvisational skills, can make all the difference for how you prepare for the audition. Understanding the conventional or unconventional genre along with relationships between characters, even if for a brief encounter, is key.

A perfect example of a brief encounter between characters that has a lasting impact on the arc of the narrative is Viola Davis's portrayal of Donald Miller's mother in *Doubt* (2004) by John Patrick Shanley. She is part of a pivotal but very small scene in the film with Meryl Streep, who plays Sister Aloysius Beauvier. Viola Davis performs for ten minutes in the film but was nominated for an Academy Award and won. Knowing how your character contributes to the larger narrative can really be worth it.

Here are some recommended strategies to find the clues in the story that will help you understand the bigger picture of the narrative:

1. Understand the medium you're acting in (theater, film, television) to better understand how the story will be told and your role in telling it.
2. Read the breakdowns, or character descriptions, provided by the casting director for all of the characters, not just yours. You can understand the synopsis of the story quickly this way.
3. Read any stage directions related to your character so that you can identify the state of the characters and the actions they perform in the scene.
4. Look for any dialogue from other characters speaking to or about your character; this research provides important clues. Too often, actors just look at "their" lines and miss important clues in the lines of other characters.
5. Read and interpret all punctuation, grammar, and syntax. Look up every word you do not know and pay close attention to punctuation and word pronunciation.
6. Pay attention to the placement of your character in the scene. Sometimes playwrights and screenwriters write people of the global majority not as three-dimensional people but as plot devices. If you understand the function of your character, you can use it to your advantage to add nuance and depth to your performance.
7. Make sure you know what happens in the beginning, middle, and end of the story that you are playing in the sides. Even when you have the whole script, you can only play one page at a time, but knowing as much as you can about the full story can inform your choices page to page.

Remember, plays, films, and TV shows are stories. The primary distinction between each platform is how the story is told. Understanding the medium for which you are auditioning and your role in the storytelling process can help you land the role.

Many mainstream acting foundations that derive from actor, director, and acting teacher Konstantin Stanislavsky's approaches to acting focus on playing actions as if they are disconnected from the story and the emotions that the characters experience in the story.[1] Such approaches can conflict with worldview and negatively impact performance in auditions. For example, like many actors in actor-training programs throughout the United States, we were both trained in Stanislavsky-based systems of acting and Black performance traditions. However, in both auditions and booked roles, we have too often been encouraged to disconnect from our own emotions as well as our gender and racial identities as Black women and people of the global majority. Such directions are counterproductive. We recognize that our bodies have a history that is connected to emotion, to our experiences, to our hopes and our dreams. We bring these feelings to the characters we play, but we have to sort out what the character is feeling in a given moment and not solely rely on those emotions in our work because they may be unreliable and volatile if we have not managed them or dealt with them. Playing actions in scenes, which is fundamental to Stanislavsky-based works, can help you identify the structures and mechanics of a story as a technician, but you don't have to deny your personal history and instincts to achieve the objective of a believable performance. You and your interpretation of the story are the most important assets that you can bring to the audition process.

When you hear acting coaches and professors talk about technique, most often they are referring to the actor's process: how they learn how to break down a script so that they can use their bodies and voices to play a character. While we do not have enough time to teach you all of the "hows" of acting in this audition book, we can offer a few recommended techniques distilled from a range of approaches to acting that can help you refine how you break down scripts in the audition room and in your everyday practice. For maximum benefit, a more detailed course of study in selected programs from the resource list in the appendix may help.

We have used these techniques in different schools, cities, and countries, and we have plenty of students who can tell you that the techniques work for them. We have successfully placed students on stages, in films, and on television shows across networks and streaming platforms using these same approaches. However, we hope that you will use the techniques to seek out additional training opportunities that will allow you to develop your practice as an actor.

If something you are doing as an actor does not feel good to you, you have to ask yourself why you are still doing it. It is not healthy to use an acting technique that "works" yet hurts you mentally, physically, or emotionally. Our approach to learning the story here is asking you to take your time to learn the "who, what, when, where, why, how" of the story. It helps to know and appreciate your own story, as discussed in chapter 2. We also want to center you, as a person of the global majority, in the story and to encourage you to follow your instincts. Only you know how you would respond within the given circumstances of the script. When you consent to audition for a work, you consent to play the content. So play it with integrity and confidence.

If you're going to judge it or seek to edit it through your performance, think twice about going to the audition. The audition room is not the place to prove a point, or to decide that the role is not worthy of your talent or consideration.

Once you understand where you are in your story and where the character is in the text, all of the lines and action will come to you that will truthfully produce the emotional moments in the character's story.

Even in preparing to play the action, it is important to leave room for spontaneity. If, as an actor, you have "tells"—like poker tells— that tip your hand to the casting directors that you know that something is about to happen in the story before it does, you ruin the suspended disbelief that you work to build for those in the room who are considering hiring you. For example, if you are bracing for a kick before it lands, you are not in the moment. Therefore, when you are talking in person or on camera for a taped audition (or self-tape), you must consider the following elements of the story:

1. Who are you in the scene? A brother, sister, wife? A worker, a lawyer?
2. What is your power relationship to the other characters with whom you reference or interact? Are you the richest, the hungriest, the weakest? Once you know your position in the scene, don't forget it. If you are extremely confident but you are auditioning for a role of a character who is not confident, you cannot let your personality bleed into your character.
3. When does the story take place? Are there time shifts? What country, city, or state is your character in? Will those discoveries require you to change your voice, dialect, cadence? All of this work has to be done before you get to the audition (i.e., job interview) so that you can ask the proper questions before you begin your reading (e.g., *Would you like me to do this with a Southern accent? I notice this takes place in Atlanta in 1969; how heavy of an accent would you like?*).
4. What is your role in the story? As a person of color who is written into the story, how is your racial identity factored into the story, if at all? In many cases, actors of the global majority are cast to add "diversity" to a predominantly White cast. In other scenarios, the racial or ethnic identity of the character is integral to the story. For example, if you are auditioning for a period piece about Booker T. Washington or Zora Neale Hurston, the racial identities of those historic figures were integral to their social and cultural perspectives and also speak to race relations in the historical moment of the work. These are clues and factors that haunt the audition process before it begins. We don't ask you to forget about your race or your culture and to focus on technique alone, like most acting teachers do, whether they be people of the global majority or White artists. We ask you to tap into the richness of yourself and your cultural experiences and use it as a contextual map to help you access the unique insights that you and

only you and your cultural experiences can bring into the room to play every character.

5. How can you be as specific as possible in your choices based on what you read in the script? How can you plan to make that specific choice that you have decided to play step by step in the room? Getting out of your head to play the specific actions and ideas that you understand in clear and succinct ways is your goal. Don't overcomplicate things with extra movements, eye rolls, deep breaths, or other extraneous gestures. Play what you planned and stick to it. When you get in the room and freestyle, you signal to the casting director that you don't know what you are doing. Ultimately, you are performing an idea of the character while revealing to the casting director that you are "performing" the part and not living in the character.

6. What would happen if your character left the scene? Would there be dramatic tension? Is your character's entrance or exit integral to the story? Does your character give or withhold valuable information?

7. How will your character get what they want in the story? If they want to be loved, how do you try to make other characters love you? What do you do to inspire their love? Identifying actions comes easily when you know how to pinpoint where the writer has left clues for how the characters pursue what they want in the story.

All of these clues in the story help you to determine your value to the scene. Once you can pinpoint your role in the story and what you are doing at a given moment, you begin to understand the stakes of your relationships and engagement in that particular scene. You will be able to find nuances and times for listening between lines that make your character's conversation appear authentic and natural as it pertains to the familiarity of the relationship.

For example, if you are playing a coffee barista in a scene, your awareness and performance are much different if your character becomes the principal love interest for the main character than if you are just there to serve coffee. Both roles require you to make choices in the room that demonstrate the character's part in the story. Overplaying your part when you're auditioning for a small role is a rookie mistake. Play your position. Don't make the role bigger or smaller than it is written. Do and say what is on the page. Don't use the part to "show" the casting director that you can "do" more. The work of the actor is to identify all of the clues in the text and to then stick them together to make us believe that you are the character on the page come to life before our eyes.

You have to appear so comfortable and easy with the text that the person you become in the room is the closest imagining of the character that the casting director has seen. This is the true art of booking the callback that gets you the job. Using your body and your voice to paint pictures of human exchange that have been sketched out for you by a playwright or screenwriter is the amazing work that actors do. Savor and enjoy it *in the audition*.

When you technically and intellectually can answer these questions using the text before your audition, you are infinitely more prepared to go in the room with strong and informed choices that inspire conversation. Conversation inspires positive reactions, and positive reactions from your auditioners in the room often result in a callback and booking.

Casting directors are looking for qualified and skilled artists, so you should treat auditions like job interviews. Doing your very best in the room every time you are invited to audition should be read as a business meeting and not a life-altering opportunity. When you go to a job interview, you don't shower your interviewer with emotion and quips such as, "This is so amazing. I really hope I get this job because this is my dream." You present confidently, thank the interviewer professionally, and leave the best impression that you can. Sending a thank-you card to the casting director referencing the opportunity goes a long way in highlighting your professionalism and business acumen.

Let your light shine when you walk into the audition room. Every job interview in acting is an interview for multiple jobs in acting. Casting directors will remember your preparedness and will call you back until your physical look and extremely thoughtful and pre-pared acting choices marry in the perfect storm that exists in the director's imagination. So be prepared for every opportunity.

To recap, what does it mean to understand a story? The way that we understand a story is directly influenced by how we see the world and the places where we live. If you have no knowledge of what it is like to live in a housing tenement in France, then it will be very difficult for you as an actor to tell that story unless you can find a connection to it (and it does not have to be personal). You don't have to speak French or visit France to play the role (unless those skills are specified in the breakdown), but you do have to know something about the culture of France in the given time period and how your character moves and thinks. Highlighting the clues in the script can help you shape the contours of your performance.

Because actors are so focused on learning their lines and memorizing the text, it is very difficult for them to tell you what a story is about in one line because as soon as they lose track of the lines, they lose track of the story. This is why it is very challenging for actors to play actions without understanding the story because they are "doing" things in the scene that are connected to lines, but not to the bigger story. Instead of working to convince the director or the casting director that you are "intense" or "into it" or "strong," work instead to understand how the actions and the emotions that the character is experiencing in your sides are connected to what the character is doing as a real, live person.

Think of a script as a score of music and the words in the script as notes. In order for actors to play—really play—a script, they have to identify the story that is in the music of the lines and use their bodies and voices to connect the notes to play a story that we want to hear. The auditioning actor is expected to perform the scene in character regardless of whether or not the reader performs or simply reads the lines of dialogue without any emotion or emphasis.

Many would-be actors think that just reading the lines loudly—with conviction and some emotion—is acting. Talking loudly and with some randomly identified emotion is not acting. It is emoting. These acts of performance are simply presentational. In everyday life, you are listening and reacting to the circumstances and the people around you. You take time to think. You absorb the environment. You make decisions based on what a person says, and then you react—or conceal your reaction to what you have heard. These are the nuances of acting.

Our racial, ethnicity, class, gender, sexuality, and ability are directly connected to how we interpret text, and that expands rather than limits the possibilities for performance. To ask an actor to divorce themselves from those intersectional realities to prove they can act is a form of violence that is simply traumatic. What is the point of directing an actor to ignore being Black, Latinx, Asian, or Native American when they are playing Willy Loman, a character who is written as a middle-aged, White, Jewish man? Recognizing the variations of how that story would play out according to these myriad identities broadens the possibilities for interpretation and translation of what it means to strive in a society as a person with restricted access.

While we firmly believe in the necessity of culturally specific work by and about people of the global majority, we recognize that many actors of the global majority will be invited to audition for the "ethnic version" of so-called classics like *Death of a Salesman* (1949) by Arthur Miller. In either case, AGM must be bold and strong enough to make choices that consider how your body, voice, and identity come to shape your interpretation of the story. Once you have the story in your body and your voice, you have to process, contextualize, and visualize yourself in the story.

To process the story essentially means to take the information you have gathered and go through the necessary steps to better understand the depth and nuance of what you have discovered and how it relates to your character. Processing the story might involve thinking about the information; talking about it with a peer, collaborator, or friend; or writing about what the information means to you as an artist and to the character within their given circumstances. You may begin to explore how to convey certain meanings through the dialogue in accent, tone, rhythm, and timing, or movement and gesture. After you process, you must contextualize the story.

To contextualize the story, you take information from the script and your research and begin to flesh it out with additional information about the sociohistorical aspects of the story that you can capture and execute in your performance (see chapter 7 for specific recommendations). It may help to know the significance of the wide-legged stance of the pachucos in the 1940s, for example, if auditioning for something like Luis Valdez's play *Zoot Suit* (1979). An understanding of the fashion of the era and how even a particular type of shoe contributes to one's stance and gait can become character traits executed in performance. Understanding the historical moment of the work, especially in the sides (which could be flashbacks or fast-forwards to different time periods), could make a huge difference in the choices you make in the moment. Now, see yourself in the story.

Once you have all of the information about the factors external to yourself (e.g., the script, the sides, the character, the relationships, the historical research, etc.), you have to visualize yourself as the character. How can you most effectively use your particular instrument—your body—to portray this character using all of the information you have gathered? What adjustments might you make to fully capture the essence of the character with the given circumstances of your instrument? If the character is described as sexy or strong or wise, what aspects of yourself can you bring into the performance to convey those things, whether or not your instrument conforms to popularized representation standards? How do your voice, body, and emotional flexibility help you execute the performance? These are all things you can practice beforehand if you prepare by reading whatever materials you can access to learn the story and your character's role within it. You have to know what your character sounds like and how they hear and respond to what is being said to them in a given moment. Things you want to consider are nationality, ethnicity, region, socioeconomic class, historical moment, race, culture, gender, and so on. All of this can contribute to the general sound of your character. But given circumstances can also indicate shifts.

So it's important to understand where your sides are placed within the larger context of the story: What happened just before the scene depicted in the sides, and how does your character feel about it? How would it affect the way they would engage and who they are engaging?

CONCLUSION

You must tell the story in its original form (don't translate it into your ideas) in a convincing manner, unless you are specifically asked to do an improvisation. In telling the story in its original form, stick to the script and any directions provided about how to conduct yourself in character. Always be prepared to bring additional flavor using the information you have gleaned from the script, sides, and contextualizing research in the event you are asked to improvise. But remember, you are still riffing off of what is already there, not inventing the character anew from random choices.

You must know who you are, where you are, who you are talking to, what they are saying to you, what you are doing, how you are doing it, and what the stakes are in the scene.

Again, you must rely on the script for the basic understanding of the character. Knowing who you are means knowing more than just your character's name. You have to learn as much as you can about who that character is according to their given circumstances, as well as who the other characters think your character is. Sometimes their views do not align, and knowing that gives you an opportunity to play subtle nuances that could set you apart from other actors. Knowing that your character, for instance, is believed to be solely an English speaker but also speaks Spanish can provide an opportunity in a selected scene to perhaps speak some of the dialogue in Spanish if it fits the situation. These can be risky choices, but if they are rooted in the script and the character the writer wrote, it will demonstrate a greater understanding of the character and highlight abilities that you can bring to the role.

Knowing where you are and who you are talking to can inform your choices. If you are at a basketball game having an argument with a partner, it would be a very different situation than arguing at home. So pay close attention to the setting of the scene in your sides; try to have a sense of where the characters just came from, where they are now, and where they are going in the next scene. All of this can inform your choices in a given scene.

Make sure you pay close attention to the other person's lines, not just as cue lines, but as valuable information about who your character is and how you feel about them. It would be a big mistake to only pay attention to your lines because you need to know what you are responding to and also what response or reaction you are trying to get out of the other person. This includes what you are doing. If you are trying to negotiate a deal with someone in a boardroom versus trying to make dinner during a strained conversation about the mortgage with your partner, it will yield a very different tone. So look for clues about stage business in the script or summary, and if none are provided, consider what you might be doing based on the context clues about what is happening between the characters.

To understand the stakes of the scene, you need to know what your character wants and is willing to do to get it from the other person in the scene. You should position yourself to be in the running for a callback when (1) you can use our map to find all of the clues in the story, (2) you can answer all of these questions clearly with defined actions to play and a deliberate physical map of the transitions and emotional shifts in the scene, and (3) within your physical map, you can also show your auditioners the physical expectations of the character with confidence and affirmation of who you are as an amazing person of the global majority.

READ THE STORY, NOT THE LINES—JOURNAL PROMPTS

Please respond to these prompts in your journal:

1. Write down a story you heard or told in your childhood. It can be a fairytale, folktale, short story, or family story.
2. Recite it out loud two times. The first time, recite from rote memory without emphasis. The second time, tell the story convincingly, providing emphasis where needed. Make a note of the difference in the retelling in your voice, body, and emotional expression.
3. Is the original version of the story realism or nonrealism? How does the telling of the story change when told in a realistic form versus a nonrealistic form?
4. Is the role you are auditioning for in theater, film, television, or some other platform? Make a note of the key elements you need to keep in mind in the storytelling based on the medium (e.g., stage performance may require greater projection and physicality compared to screen performance, which through the use of cameras and microphones may allow for speaking in softer tones and less dramatic physicality).
5. Review the breakdown, sides, and any information provided about the story. In your own words:

   a. Write a summary of the story of the work you are auditioning for, and make a note of where the sides take place in the larger story and how your character fits into the larger scheme of the story.
   b. Answer the *who, what, when, where, why,* and *how* questions for your character, and note the relationship with the character(s) sharing the scene based on the information you are provided. What is at stake in the scene? *(Note:* Any research you do can help flesh out what is on the page and should be anchored in the story.)
   c. Make a list of key character traits, directions, given circumstances, and story elements you can play in performance.

6. Practice telling the story by scaffolding the information you gathered into your performance each time you practice the sides as written or improvised. What do you discover about your character in the process?

7. Identify key lines spoken about you by other characters, including the context in which the line is delivered. Note how your character feels about that person and how you can portray that in performance in verbal and nonverbal ways (make a list of possible options).

8. After each of these steps, write a single sentence or phrase that names what your character wants and from whom. Consider why and how they plan to get it. This will help you convincingly play your part in telling the story.

4

PLAY PUNCTUATION AND PRACTICE PRONUNCIATION

Why have a chapter on auditioning that addresses punctuation? Could you all just get to the good stuff?

This is the good stuff. This is the gold! Punctuation is a technical tool used by the writer to guide the actor as to how the writer hears the line in the story. Playwrights, screenwriters, and all other writers use punctuation to create clarity, intention, and meaning in a sentence.

If you think that learning lines and presenting as "memorized" is the key to auditioning, you will become an "auditioner," rather than a working actor who actually books roles. Sounds harsh, but it's true. As working actors and directors who teach actors how to audition, we hope this book can help center you, a person of the global majority, in the work of auditioning. Language usage plays an important role in the process, thus the focus on pronunciation and punctuation as a key element of breaking it down for auditions.

Punctuation, as a process of shaping a sentence in the tone and intention of the writer, is racialized, although it can be repeated or revised by the speaker. As linguistic studies of African American vernacular English demonstrate, language is connected to worldview. Grammar, syntax, and sentence structure factor into representations of culture, race, and worldview through speech. So when a

White writer uses punctuation in a way that captures the tone, pacing, and audacity of the White characters they write for, they are also capturing the associated worldview. If they do not draw from actual linguistic patterns of the culture being represented, rather than stereotypical approximations, they are reinforcing White supremacy through Eurocentric worldviews while using people of the global majority as cover. Too often, White writers who are writing about "people of color" will either write global majority characters with the same speech patterns as the White characters or attempt to write how they think this "character of color" speaks instead of drawing from actual linguistic patterns that may be more familiar to cultural insiders.

If you're auditioning for a TV show or web series, understand that there is a team of writers from all different racial and ethnic groups—too often majority white—working on the scripts for each episode. Therefore, when you meet a character of color on the page, keep these things in mind:

1. The character may not sound or act like you think a person of the global majority would because the character on the page is an amalgamation of many ideas that are distilled by the writers into the voice of a single character. We have to fight for specificity of representation and use our knowledge to illuminate those specificities in the room when we are presenting the character in the audition.

2. Nine times out of ten, the language of characters of color in plays, television, and film projects that are written by predominantly White writers and are written to be played by predominantly White casts will usually not have any racial or ethnic specific characteristics besides a few lines that indicate their racial identity through the use of vernacular or other presentational attributes.

3. Do not assume that because you represent a particular racial or ethnic group, you will be fluent in a group's various vernaculars, speech patterns, cultural references, and so on. You have to treat the speech and language of people of the global

majority as specifically as you would any Eurocentric "elevated" or "vernacular" speech. Just because you are African American does not mean that you will be able to successfully play someone who is Jamaican because you and the character share Black racial identity. This rule holds for all people of the global majority. Race, ethnicity, and nationality are all shaped by gender, class, and sexuality. So do your homework and do not make assumptions because, in many cases, your auditioners will not have the cultural literacy to make these distinctions and will just call you in to audition because they see you as generically Black, Latinx, Asian, Native, Indigenous, Arab, and so on, based on your résumé, headshots, and reel.

4. Writers from the global majority who are writing characters of specific racial and ethnic backgrounds are also using punctuation and pronunciation to capture how they want the character to sound. Sometimes this writing may also conform to Eurocentric expectations in order to even get to production. Mainstream reviewers of plays, television shows, and films, who are predominantly White (thus, we need more critics from the global majority, please!), often discuss the use of language (and therein punctuation) of the writer as "innovative," "interesting," or "authentic," which is just code to say the writers do not write or speak in Standard American or British English. No to that. Writers of color are just as educated, brilliant, "universal," and any other amazing adjective used to describe White writers. Because so many actors have been trained in Eurocentric traditions, many are led to devalue the writing and language use of non-White writers. It is high time to face and revise those problematic assumptions.

5. If you are a person of color approaching "White text" (i.e., text that was not written about, by, for people of the global majority), you may have to do some intention and translation work when you approach certain texts, especially when considering speech patterns of characters. The punctuation use of the writer gives you clues as to how the character speaks. If

the writer is writing in vernacular and there are no commas or other punctuation save periods, they may be indicating that this character talks fast and does not have a lot of breath in the line. Think Kia Corthron's plays.

6. Learning basic punctuation marks can help you identify the pacing and rhythm of a text. The more fluent you are in the usage of each punctuation mark, the easier it is for you to be able to interpret the line as written. For example, punctuation in Shakespeare's plays serves a rhetorical function, not purely a grammatical one. Shakespeare's works contain specific punctuation. The use of commas, semicolons, and other punctuation marks indicates lengths of pauses and implied stage action for the director and actor. By using punctuation to block scenes, Shakespeare implies how lines could be performed. However, in some cases, particularly in the work of writers of the global majority, punctuation rules that pertain to European-derived languages are often subverted. Equally important to note is that global majority writers may adhere to Eurocentric punctuation norms appropriate for the language that they write in, so a rule of thumb is not to assume and to play what is on the page. Period. Pun intended.

7. In order to understand these moments of rebellion, you actually have to know the rules that are being broken by the playwright or screenwriter. The rules that we discuss in this chapter can be used to interpret all of the punctuation explanations in most straight plays written by writers who use English as the primary language of their characters. In most cases, punctuation is not only used to meet grammatical requirements for English but also may be used to disrupt these norms to create specific rhythms and disruptions in the play. For example, in her work, poet and playwright Ntozake Shange intentionally breaks Standard American English grammar and punctuation rules to, in her words, "attack deform n maim the language that i waz taught to hate myself in," which results in a particular musicality on the page.[1] In these sentences, it is important to know the grammatical rules so that you can rec-

ognize when the author is breaking them. In some instances, you are not getting a callback because your performance of the punctuation in the room has changed the meaning of the story.

8. Speak the speech: Don't judge the character's way of speaking or doing; just do what is written on the page. Play what is written. We've all played a line of dialogue and changed the meaning of the text in an audition by running over periods, not pausing at commas, or not emphasizing important information given by the writer after colons. There are specific vocal and physical possibilities embedded in the punctuation of the lines. Learning them will help you map physical actions and learn more about how your character is feeling in a scene.

So, in short, please pay attention to punctuation in every line of dialogue.

There are fourteen basic punctuation symbols that are vital for any actor to understand and can help them break down a script. Here we offer basic definitions and examples and recommend that you buy a basic English grammar book (select American or British English depending on usage) to familiarize yourself with the rules so that you understand more of the intent of the playwright or screenwriter when you are given a script. If English is not your first language, we suggest that you buy the dictionary of the language that your script is in to make sure that you understand the intention of the lines and all of the words in the script. Just because you think you know how to pronounce a word does not mean that is the way that it is pronounced, so be sure. One of the authors here (okay, Nicole) lost a recurring role on a series because she mispronounced a word, and it drove the producers crazy, so they did not cast her.

The whole point of focusing on punctuation and pronunciation is to make sure that you understand in auditions that punctuation sets the pacing and intention of a line for a writer. When you disrespect the punctuation and pronunciation as if "it didn't really matter," you are in effect telling the writer that you are not a big follower of rules and that you could not care less about the details of the script or the meaning of the story. Casting directors are looking for professionals to fill the roles they are casting, so if you break the rules early on for no apparent reason, what you are communicating to the casting director and the director is that you do not pay attention to detail and will not invest the necessary energy and effort in the storytelling.

Punctuation symbols give the English language (as well as most European Slavic and Romance languages) a roadmap of intentions that gives us the closest approximation to the original intent of the author. In African, Asian, Indigenous, and other non-Western languages, you must also consider punctuation, but more so in a holistic context of the cultural usages of pauses, breath, silences, wordless utterances, and other details over time that are embedded in the symbols, script, and/or sounds of the language.

This book addresses global majority artists working in primarily English-speaking markets in the United States and Europe, so our focus is on Western uses of punctuation. For example, symbols in African languages such as Yoruba and Swahili are important to understanding stresses and intonation. Similar marks of punctuation are used in Arabic and Hebrew. We cannot address all of the punctuation rules for non-English usage for non-Western languages here. However, we encourage you to follow the same rules as specified for each language and to obey all punctuation indications in the script as written by the playwright or screenwriter. Knowing the rules in non-Western languages may help when playing various accents in English.[2]

Punctuation gives you clues to how the character feels and how they form their thoughts in the world of the play, television show, or film. To ignore a comma or a set of ellipses is to ignore how the line is crafted by the writer and therefore the tone, mood, and meaning imagined for the character in the moment. You have to play the pauses, the stops, the backslashes. Everything. All of the parts of a script are like puzzle pieces or musical notes written by the writer. In the audition, it's your job as an actor to play them as conceived and written by the writer unless *you are instructed to ignore* the punctuation by the casting director in the audition or the director on set.

SENTENCE ENDINGS

The punctuation marks most commonly used in writing to end lines of speech are the period, the question mark, and the exclamation point.

The period is most often placed at the end of complete thoughts, declarative sentences, and most abbreviations.

- As a sentence ender: *Paul said that he was sure.*
- After an abbreviation: *Linda's son, Paul, was born on Jan. 5, 2020.*

Question marks are used to mark a direct or rhetorical question when placed at the end of a sentence. Actors' intonation may rise at the end of a question mark or can often be "thrown away" to indicate that the question is rhetorical.

- Direct question: *What time is the dinner tonight?*
- Possible rhetorical interpretation: *Do you think I'm crazy or something?*

Beware of unconsciously slipping into twenty-first-century speech patterns such as "upspeak," in which the speaker ends sentences with a rising inflection even if the sentence is not a question. This is frequently an unconscious habit that you should be mindful of, as it can alter the meaning of the writing or simply annoy the casting director and director if it is not a speech pattern associated with the character.

Exclamation points are used when a character expresses anger, emphasizes a point, or is yelling.

- Within dialogue: *"What the hell!" she yelled.*

- To emphasize a point: *Your lies are the source of the problems!*

Take a look at this excerpt from the Lena Waithe television show *Twenties* (2020) for usage of exclamation points within dialogue and point emphasis:

INT. MARIE AND CHUCK'S APARTMENT—LATER THAT
NIGHT
Post dinner. The lights have been dimmed, candles have been lit,
and Kendrick Lamar is in the background rapping about God and
what it means to be a free black man. Everyone sits around the
table, including BEN, Marie's co-worker. He's the OJ of executives, and LAUREN —his well-meaning white girlfriend.

MARIE
I can't believe you tweeted that.

HATTIE
I believe she stalked my Twitter page.

NIA
I know!

MARIE
She did what any woman in her position is supposed to do.

LAUREN
What happened?

BEN
Ida found some shady tweets Hattie wrote about "Cocoa's Butter."

LAUREN
Oh my God I love that show!
Everyone cuts their eyes at her. She cowers.

HATTIE
It's cool, I ain't want that job no way.

MARIE
You wanna know what your problem is?

HATTIE
I don't actually.

MARIE
You don't know what you want.

                        HATTIE
                I want to be a writer.
                        MARIE
    That can't be true, because if you did you would be writing
    every day. If you wanted to be a writer you'd be at the WGA
    [Writers Guild of America] reading scripts cover to cover!
                    MARIE (CONT'D)
    If you wanted to be a writer you wouldn't be tweeting shady shit
     about a popular black show you could potentially work on.
                        HATTIE
                Don't talk to me like I'm a child.
                        MARIE
                Then stop acting like one!
                         NIA
    Sisters! We are not doing this on my birthday! Both of you need
                to take a breath. [3]

Marie and Nia do as they're told. Everyone looks a little shell-
shocked.

In this scene from *Twenties,* the exclamation points are used to
mark various emotional outbursts or attacks that friends engage in
during a birthday dinner conversation. Making sure to follow the
volley of comments and who is talking to whom will let the actor
know when and how to place the emphasis on the exclamation
points when it is their character's turn to speak. Similarly, you can
track the comma usage in the above scene to understand the imagined pacing for the line as written.

The comma, semicolon, and colon are common punctuation
marks that we engage almost every day. All of these marks can be
used to indicate a pause in a series of thoughts, ideas, things, experiences, and so on.

The comma is used by the writer to separate ideas or elements
within a sentence. Commas are also used in dialogue to directly
address someone, as well as to separate thoughts, numbers, and
dates. Commands are also used in opening salutations and the separation of thoughts.

- Direct address: *Thanks for all your advice, Hattie.*
- Separation of two complete sentences (with coordination conjunction—*for, and, nor, but, or, yet*): *We went to the mall, and then we went out to the movies.*
- Separating lists or elements within sentences: *I want the soup, salad, and half sandwich, please.*

It should be noted that the use of a comma before the conjunction in a list is often a point of style choice. This final comma, known as an Oxford or serial comma, is used in a complex series of elements or phrases, but in some styles (e.g., British English as well as U.S. journalism), it is often considered unnecessary in a simple series. For example:

- Oxford comma: *Deondre shared the engagement announcement, champagne, and breakfast with his parents.*
- No Oxford comma: *He shared the engagement announcement, champagne and breakfast with his parents.*

The semicolon (;) connects dependent clauses. It is used to establish a closer relationship between the clauses than a period would show. *Ian is happy now; I knew he had to accept his fate.*

A colon (:) has three main uses. The first usage is after a word introducing a quotation, an explanation, an example, or a series.

- *She was planning to buy four skin care products: face scrub, moisturizer, toner, and a mask.*

The second usage is between independent clauses when the second explains the first, similar to a semicolon:

- *I didn't have time to chat: I was already late.*

The third use of a colon is for emphasis:

- *There was one thing I wanted more than anything: a fresh start.*

If you follow the rules of each usage, you can see how you may interpret the emphasis of a line very differently than if you ignored the punctuation altogether. In the example above, the emphasis of the line should be placed after the colon. Many actors would read it as one sentence with no emphasis on delineation. The emphasis of the line as written by the author is on the second component after "There was one thing I wanted more than anything." To read the line as a complete thought with no consideration of the colon means that you have misunderstood part of the line and neglected to verify that the actor reading and the character has understood the meaning of the sentence.

THE DASH AND THE HYPHEN

The dash and the hyphen are two other important punctuation marks. These marks are often confused with each other due to their appearance, but they are very different. A dash is used to separate words into statements. There are two common types of dashes: en dash and em dash.

- En dash: Think of the en dash (–) as a double hyphen, so to speak. The en dash (–) is used to indicate a range or between time, locations, ideas, objects, and so on: *1910 – 1925* or *Paris – Amsterdam trains*.
- Em dash: The em dash (—) is even longer than the en dash. The em dash (—) can be used in place of a parenthesis, a comma, or even a colon to make a sentence flow and to high-light the conclusion of a sentence. Here is an example from *Contribution* (1969) by Ted Shine: "You ain't gonna get no wounds, son, and you ain't gonna get this nice white shirt ruined either. What's wrong with you anyway? You tryin' to—what y'all say—'chicken out'?"[4]

A hyphen (-) is used to join two or more words together into a compound term and is not separated by spaces. For example, *part-time*, *back-to-back*, *well-known*.

When you meet these punctuation marks in dialogue marked for your character, please take time to examine each mark and remember what the mark is illuminating to you about your character's speech patterns, thought patterns, cadences, accents, and experiences. Also keep in mind that speech patterns generally reflect worldviews and, as demonstrated in chapter 3, may help you effectively use language to play the character with greater variation, depth, and nuance. In *Limitations of Life* (1938), Langston Hughes uses skits to satirize the portrayal of Blacks in Hollywood's film industry.[5] Here we have a line from the character "Mammy" which is a parody of the mother character in the film *Imitation of Life* (1935), starring Claudette Colbert and Fredi Washington, the story of a White woman who takes in a Black nanny and her daughter to live with her and her daughter. The Black woman's daughter tries to pass as White.

> Audette: Lawd? Mammy Weavers, ma little Riola's tryin' so hard to be colored. She just loves Harlem. . . .
>
> Mammy: What a shame. The darling's so fair and blue-eyed! Even though her father *was* an Eskimo, you'd never know it. *Never*.[6]

Here, Langston Hughes uses the hyphen to create the word *blue-eyed*. The actor should pronounce it as one word, not two.

BRACKETS, BRACES, AND PARENTHESES

Brackets are the squared-off notations ([]) used for technical explanations or to clarify meaning. If you remove the information in the brackets, the sentence will still make sense. If you meet brackets in a line of dialogue, the information in the brackets is for the actor and should not be spoken out loud.

- *She [Professor Hannigas] was the last person seen with the student.*

Braces ({}) are used to connect two or more lines of text or listed items to show that they should be considered a unit. They are not commonplace in theater or screenplays, but can be seen in mathematical expressions and computer-programming language. For example, if you had a line of dialogue that read as follows:

Marcia: The equation $2\{1+[23-3]\} = x$ is what we are attempting to solve this afternoon.

You would have to call out the brackets in reading the line of dialogue to help the audience understand how to write the equation out in their mind's eye. Think of a show like *Proof* (2000) by David Auburn, or the films *Good Will Hunting* (1997) by Ben Affleck and Matt Damon and *Hidden Figures* (2016) by Melfi and Alison Schroeder, where mathematical equations figure heavily in the character dialogue. Brackets of various kinds are also used in scripts to indicate that the line will be translated into another language or spoken by an actor who will be hired and will translate the line from English to the desired language. The text in the brackets in your script is what will be subtitled in English. A reproduction of a page from the script from the short-lived Netflix show *Messiah* (2020) created by Michael Petroni serves as an example of how these type of brackets may be used.

"MESSIAH" 101 "HE THAT HATH AN EAR" WRITER'S FOURTH DRAFT
8-15-17

A man steals the shoes from a sleeping woman's feet—or perhaps she's dead.

Thousands of hungry eyes stare vacantly. Awaiting food relief that will not reach them.

The distant, persistent CLATTER OF GUNFIRE fills the air.

We move over the desperate faces to find JIBRIL (16)—hungry and helpless like every other soul around him. On his lap, his MOTHER lays her head . . . her eyes closed.

Looking down at her, concern clouds his expression. . . .

> JIBRIL
> (Arabic: subtitled)
> <Mother . . .>

He gently nudges her shoulder. . . .

> JIBRIL(CONT'D)
> <Mother . . .>

He touches her cheek . . . she does not move.

He opens one of her eyes carefully with his fingers—it stares lifelessly back at him.

From the pain in Jibril's eyes—

CUT TO:

INT. JIBRIL'S MOTHER'S BEDROOM—FLASHBACK

DARKNESS.

We hear the soft padding of footsteps. . . .

A small bedside LIGHT SWITCHES ON illuminating the face of Jibril's Mother—she is younger, and sleeping. She opens her eyes, woken by the light, and looks kindly at her son Jibril (WHO IS 7 YEARS OLD IN THIS MEMORY), standing by her bed, his eyes full of fear.

JIBRIL
<I had a nightmare.>

Without a word she lifts her blankets and lets him crawl into her bed—snuggling . . . hoping she is enough to comfort him.

Parentheses (()) are used to contain or bracket thoughts that the playwright or screenwriter wants to communicate to the actor or the director. The parentheses contain further thoughts communicated by the author that can help the actor understand the relationships between the characters. In most instances (except parenthetical citations of authors, etc.), parentheses can be replaced by commas without changing the meaning. For example, in the sentence below, we learn new information about the characters in the parentheses.

- *John and Jane (who are actually half brother and sister) both have red hair.*

Parentheses are also used to give you information about the action performed by or the emotional or physical state of the characters. In this scene from *How to Get Away with Murder* (2014) created by Shonda Rhimes, the parenthetical information shows the actor what they should be "doing" in the scene and how they should respond to certain dialogue.

INT. DEAN'S HOUSE—NIGHT 30 A COCKTAIL PARTY.
Our 1Ls are dressed up, downing champagne and mixing with PROFESSORS. Wes arrives at the front door, greeted by the liquored-up DEAN OF THE LAW SCHOOL and his BORED WIFE.

DEAN OF THE LAW SCHOOL
Welcome! Dean Howard. This is my wife, Constance.
WES
Wes Gibbins. Thank you so much for—
Before Wes can finish, the Dean moves to the next arriving
student.
DEAN OF THE LAW SCHOOL
Welcome! Dean Howard. This is my wife, Constance.
Across the room, Wes spots Patrick, Michaela, and Doucheface
talking to TOM (40s, handsome, friendly). Tom is a breath of
fresh air in this competitive environment—positive, encourag-
ing, nice even.
As Wes joins . . .

TOM
First year's the worst, no doubt. Just put your head down, do the
work, and try not to take it so seriously.
DOUCHEFACE
You're obviously not a lawyer.
TOM
A psychology professor. I know, you've just lost all respect for
me, but I work with the firm sometimes—evaluating clients,
reading witnesses. (noticing Wes) And you are?
PATRICK
This is Wes, Tom. He's in your wife's class too.
TOM (shaking his hand)
How's it going so far, Wes? Has she gone full terrorist on you
yet?
WES
I'm sorry . . . who's your wife?
MICHAELA
Professor DeWitt. (to Tom, sucking up) Who, can I just say, is
literally my favorite. [7]

In this scene you learn that you have to incorporate the prescribed action for your character based on what is in the parentheses. You also have to mark who your character is talking to at any
given time. If you are talking to one person in a scene and that focus
shifts, you have to change where you are looking and acknowledge

that a shift has occurred in your audition. You map your movement based on what the action calls for in the scene you are playing.

Another important use of parentheses in playwriting and screen-writing is to use the abbreviation for "continued" after action or location description shifts to indicate that your character is still talking. Often, actors will wait to deliver the second part of the line marked by "(CONT'D)" when, in fact, they should mark their script to react to whatever is described in the action lines while picking up the continued dialogue. You should pay attention to the action in the script and connect the dots between your character's dialogue between the lines before the "(CONT'D)." Always read what is in the parentheses.

Similarly, in the plays and film scripts of Suzan-Lori Parks, the playwright uses parentheses to indicate "rests" for the actor. Parks imagines that these should mimic music rests within quotations to jump from one phrase to another, omitting unnecessary words that do not interfere with the meaning. Here is an excerpt from *The America Play* (1996), a retelling of American history from the point of view of an African American Abraham Lincoln impersonator who lives in "The Great Hole of History." Parks uses parentheses to prescribe rhythm and pacing choices for the actor playing "The Foundling Father as Abraham Lincoln."

> ACT ONE: LINCOLN ACT. A Great hole. In the middle of nowhere. The hole is an exact replica of the Great Hole of History.
> THE FOUNDLING FATHER AS ABRAHAM LINCOLN: "To stop too fearful and too faint to go."
> *(rest)*
> "He digged the hole and the whole held him."
> *(rest)*
> "I cannot dig, to beg I am ashamed."
> *(rest)*
> "He went to the theatre but home went she."
> Goatee. Goatee. What he sported when he died. It's not my favorite.
> *(rest)*

"He digged the hole and whole held." Huh.

(rest)

There was once a man who was told that he bore a strong resemblance to Abraham Lincoln. He was tall and thinly built, just the Great Man. His legs were the longer part just like the Great Mans legs. His hands and feet were large as the Great Man's were large. The Lesser Known had several beards which he carried around in a box. The beards were his although he himself had not grown them on his face but since he'd secretly bought the hairs his barber and arranged their beard shapes and since the procurement and upkeep of his beards took so much work he figured that the beards were completely his—were as authentic as he was, so to speak. His beard box was of cherry wood and lined with velvet. He had the initials "A.L." tooled in gold on the lid. *(rest)* [8]

APOSTROPHES, QUOTATION MARKS, AND ELLIPSES

The apostrophe, quotation mark, and ellipsis are distinctly different punctuation marks and cannot be used interchangeably in any form. An apostrophe (') is used to indicate the omission of a letter or letters from a word, the possessive case, or the plurals of lowercase letters. Examples include:

- Omission of letters from a word: *I've* (contraction for *I have*) *seen that man several times. He isn't the same man that is being held on bond.*
- Possessive case: *Walter's hat was left on the hat rack.*
- Lowercase letters plural: *Marika's classmates were learning their abc's.*

When you see quotation marks in a script, they can be used to indicate direct quotes attributed to another speaker or "scare quotes" (scare quotes are added to highlight to the reader to question the validity of the content that is inside the quotation frame). In some instances, actors will learn this from the context of the line, or they may have stage directions from the writer to indicate "air quotes" while speaking.

- *"Be the change that you wish to see in the word."*—Mahatma Gandhi

Single quotation marks (' ') are used to indicate that the speaker is speaking in the voice of someone else through acts of citation.

- Luis said, *"Dante is my brother, and he said to me 'Why don't you love me like you love Sister?' and I finally heard him."*

The ellipsis is most commonly represented by three periods (. . .) and is used to indicate an omission of words, ideas, thoughts, and so on. It often marks that the character is cutting off their speech for lack of further information or because they intend to be silent, gather their thoughts, or resist anger or another emotion. Ellipses are frequently used by screenwriters and playwrights to indicate that the character has come to the end of a thought and chooses not to say more. The character may elect to change the subject after ellipses. They may also have an ellipsis followed by a backslash, which indicates that their line will be cut off by the next speaker in the dialogue.

Ellipses can also be used in brackets to indicate that a citation is longer than what is quoted by the author. For example, authors quoting parts of speeches will often employ an ellipsis to avoid copying lengthy text.

An example of ellipses used to show the speech is longer than cited and the omission of words is from Beneatha's sled speech in *A Raisin in the Sun* (1958). Each dot is an ellipsis:

> Me? . . . Me? . . . Me I'm nothing. . . . Me. When I was very small . . . we used to take our sleds out in the winter time and the only hill we had were the ice covered stone steps of some houses down the street. And we used to fill them in with snow and make them smooth and slide down them all day . . . and it was very dangerous you know . . . far too steep.[9]

An example of omitting words can be found in *Wine in the Wilderness* (1969) by Alice Childress:

> No, no, they not really after me but . . . I was in the basement so I could stash this stuff . . . but a fella tole me they pokin' round down there . . . in the backyard pokin' round . . . the police doin' a lot of pokin' round. [10]

In Childress's play, we can see the way the author uses the ellipses to build momentum and weight in the delivery for the actor. With each ellipses, we see the tension build about Old Timer's anxiety about the police.

Here is an example from *Wine in the Wilderness* that shows use of parentheses within a quotation: "Slow down Old Timer, wait till you see this. There she is. . . . 'Wine in the Wilderness' . . . Mother Africa, regal, black womanhood in her noblest form."[11] When you, as the actor, encounter the quotation marks in a line, your delivery of the line should audibly (e.g., change in tone, emphasis, etc.) or physically (e.g., air quotes, etc.) let the person you are talking to in the scene hear you emphasizing what is between the quotation marks.

Backslash: If you see a backslash at the end or beginning of a line, it means that the playwright or screenwriter wants the actor with the first backslash to be cut off by the actor whose next line begins with a backslash. In most instances, the writer will tell you how to treat the backslash. If your line comes first, you should expect an actor to cut you off where the backslash appears in the line.

Here's an example from *Baybra's Tulips* (2018) by Lewis Morrow. The backslash after "I just" indicates to the character Baybra that he should not let Charles finish his line, but should cut him off. The backslash indicates to Charles that he will be cut off by the other actor, so he should be prepared to have a full thought at the end of the line so as not to appear as if his speech stops suddenly or that he has gone up on a line. (That's industry speak for forgetting a line.)

CHARLES

I asked about you all the time. Every time your sister talked to you or went to see you. I just didn't know if you wanted to see me to be honest. I mean . . . with everything that happened . . . you know . . . I just /

BAYBRA

Yeah, it's cool. Speaking of *everything*, how are you and Tellu-lah doing?

The actor playing Baybra should be prepared to cut Charles off some time before or right on the edge of his line after "I just." Also note the use of ellipses twice by the playwright to suggest that the character should fill those spaces with a projection of some emotional weight. The character does not have words to fill that gap in thought, so therefore, the actor should know how they will "fill" that space and connect the thought. The line is not written to be read in sequence, but with space in between "I mean" and "with everything that happened." The pattern reappears before the backslash line break. If your line begins with a backslash, this mark indicates you should cut the actor's line above yours at the end of the backslash in the previous sentence.

If you see several character names with backslashes, such as JARON/KEISHA/MIRELLA/DONOVAN, this means that the characters are speaking the same lines simultaneously. Take this example of simultaneous dialogue indicated by backslashes in the *How to Get Away with Murder* pilot script:

MICHAELA/PATRICK/LAUREL/WES

You should've agreed with me weeks ago when I begged, BEGGED, to tell the police instead of deluding ourselves that we were on the right side of this!/And I'm sorry Laurel but someone will sniff out the body if we bury it, if they don't catch us before, there are cops everywhere

tonight!/You two need to MAN UP and
THINK because we're going to jail
unless we go back there and destroy
the DNA!/Guys . . . Listen . . . Hey . . . SHUT
UP!

Finally they all stop, look at Wes. He's calm, focused, a quiet
and confident leader to this very outspoken group.

WES

It's two against two. We have no
other choice. We flip a coin.

Beat.

MICHAELA/PATRICK/LAUREL

That is the dumbest thing you've
ever said. /I'm not letting a
freaking coin decide this. /We're
adults, we can figure this out/ . . .

WES

We don't have time to fight! We
need to decide and commit
to it. So if someone has a better
idea say it now!

They all realize, no one does. Wes pulls a coin out of his pocket.

WES (CONT'D)

Heads we get the body. Tails we
leave it where it is. Okay? [12]

CONCLUSION

Overall, we encourage you to take time to review a punctuation
point a day for fourteen days and practice with texts written by
people of the global majority, especially those that capture the cadences that ring truest for the range of people represented within a
cultural group. In the process, you may discover alternative usages
as writers deploy a range of techniques, including but not limited to
punctuation and pronunciation, for more nuanced storytelling.

Once you understand the use of the punctuation, you will be able to break down your scripts and the rhythm of the writer's language so much faster. You will be able to identify if your character is racialized through the culture and language in the script as well as the physical characteristics described in the audition breakdown. For example, if you get a script that takes place in a suburban conservative town and your character is an African American student who is transferring to the school, you can study the punctuation and the language to find out how the character is positioned, how fast they talk, what their thought process is, and more. The punctuation reveals the secrets in the script that make visible the sonic and physical intentions of the character that are embedded in the lines.

PUNCTUATION AND PRONUNCIATION— JOURNAL PROMPTS

Please respond to these prompts in your journal:

1. What stands out to you about the punctuation used by the writer in your sides?
2. Do you understand all of the punctuation in your audition sides, scene, or monologue? Map three actions that the punctuation highlights for you.
3. How can you remind yourself to play each punctuation point in your script?
4. Write a mantra that you can say before an audition that reminds you to play what's on the page and that you are enough exactly as you are.

5

PLAYING THE ACTION

If you've never had the opportunity to study acting in a formal setting at a school, church, or community class, maybe you're not familiar with Konstantin Stanislavsky's idea of playing an action.[1] What does playing an action mean? It is very simple. In a nutshell, "playing the action" emphasizes what you are doing in the scene while in character. You have to know what your character is doing in the scene. What you are doing is directly connected to what you are feeling, which subsequently produces the emotional states of the characters and informs their interactions.

In essence, the idea comes from Konstantin Stanislavsky (1863–1938), a White, Russian artist, and later acting teacher, who developed a system of acting that merges psychology with acting technique, including but not limited to plotting out a series of actions and playing them in a sequence to trick the body into producing a particular emotional state for the performer. The practice is designed to inspire more consistent and realistic performances. The recommendations that we offer here are based on our experiences as actors, as acting teachers in university and studio classrooms, and as directors.

Popularized techniques inspired by Stanislavsky, like "emotion-memory," often suggest that if you can get your subconscious to believe that what you are doing is real, the body will respond in kind and produce "authentic" emotional experiences. Actors of the global majority, like Dr. Barbara Ann Teer, a Black woman and founder of the National Black Theatre and her own system of acting, have observed the dangers of such popularized techniques. Depending on who the actor is, and what racial, ethnic, gender, or class status they hold, certain actions do not produce desired emotional outcomes and can actually harm the actor.[2] The "one-size-fits-all" approach of the Stanislavsky traditions, which are at the foundation of most Western acting approaches in the United States, is that it assumes the actor doing the work and action playing is White and unmarked by race.

As we were both exposed to Stanislavsky-based systems in our training, we recognize the limitations and possibilities and have firsthand experience with the harm associated with these techniques. We are not saying that Stanislavsky-based systems are wrong if they work for you. But we encourage you to explore other Western and non-Western approaches to acting that center the expression and experiences of people of the global majority. We also suggest that when using Stanislavsky-based acting approaches, you can and should supplement them by drawing from acting traditions that acknowledge race, ethnicity, and gender as always already a part of the life force that an actor brings to the role and the character brings to the world of the play.

The Stanislavsky focus on playing actions as the principal way forward is centered in Eurocentric acting techniques throughout the United States. There are many other approaches that spring from other non-European traditions that are equally useful ways to deepen your approach to acting that allow you to feel the very best you can feel about performing and the craft. These approaches may not be as popular as "method" or "Meisner" or "Laban" or psychological-object-based acting in majority-White schools in the United States, Canada, and England, but that does not make them inferior.

Ignoring who the actor is and assuming that they can simply play actions and ignore the emotional and physical trauma of playing a role that was not written for a person of color is part of the institutional racism of actor-training programs internationally. From West

African griot approaches to storytelling and performance to Japanese Suzuki methods, actors of the global majority and non-global majority performers must learn as much as they can about the business of acting and cultural distinctions regardless of whether or not they are using Stanislavsky-based approaches to the work.

Playing actions is just a fancy way of telling you to know what the character is doing in the scene. What does this mean? This means if your character is reading while talking, then read. If your character is watching TV, make sure you are watching TV. If your character is avoiding having a conversation, then you avoid having the conversation. Use the lines to convey what the character is feeling and doing in the scene. When you perform with a "put on" aesthetic, not many people believe you. Have you ever watched a performance and said to yourself, "Wow, that feels fake"? Well, ten times out of ten you feel that way because what you are witnessing does not move you or ring true in any way. Trust that instinct.

If you are eating cereal as you reluctantly break up with your boyfriend, your actions can be eating and avoiding or picking at the cereal as you break the news to your boyfriend. Or, you could just simply get into the moment and pretend like you're eating some cereal and then tell the person in the scene that you don't want to be with them anymore. How you say the line is completely dependent on how you eat the cereal and where your focus is between doing that action and saying what your character is saying. You have to synthesize the action to the emotional content all while establishing a relationship with the scene partner or, in most cases, the camera lens on your smartphone that you use to record yourself so that you can submit the audition to be considered for the job.

The key is to engage in the action in a way that externalizes internal thoughts and emotions or the avoidance of those emotions rather than simply playing the emotion itself. Make no mistake, playing the action is not separate and distinct from portraying emotion, as certain actions can trigger emotional states through variations of memory (emotion memory, muscle memory, blood memory, and even cultural trauma). But simply playing "sad" may not be as believable as breaking down the action in the scene.

The more you grow as an actor, the more you will track what your process is, what helps you make sense of the relationships you are playing in a scene. We encourage you to explore the breakdown steps that we offer as a shortcut to excavating playable clues in the script. Playing actions is part of the acting technique that came out of Stanislavsky's work, but we want you to know that this is just another way of saying that you have to pretend what you are doing in the scene is what you—the actor—perceive that the person in the scene needs to do to get what they want in a given moment. When you do this from moment to moment, you are effectively "in the moment." This is key to understanding how effectively you have processed the story and responded in the same way that the character thinks and feels about the situation based on what is written on the page. Playing actions is meant to give you a wide range of choices so that you do not feel as if you are somehow stuck in portraying surface-level emotion that comes across as fake because it is disconnected from action and interaction.

If at any time you feel insecure that you cannot reproduce the same performance time after time in the same fashion, this is where technique enters the equation along with the knowledge a performance is never exactly the same but can be replicated to a certain degree through the use of technique. As a professional actor, you have to be able to repeatedly replicate a performance as consistently as possible based on the number of takes that a casting director asks you to repeat. This is a skill.

We encourage you to find time in your acting process to identify a teacher who can help you amplify your talent and desire to explore a technique that allows you to be your whole self in the pursuit of a full-time acting career. An effective acting teacher or coach can help you become adept in various acting techniques so that you become proficient. You deserve to affirm exactly who you are as an actor without having to attempt to fit yourself into the techniques and styles of performance and aesthetic that appeal to predominantly White directors and producers.

Remember, every character is doing something in a scene. Sitting quietly is doing something. Standing impatiently is doing something. Find the actions and play them as they are connected to how the character is feeling. Many acting teachers call this "psycho-physical gesture" connection. In layperson's terms, this is using the gesture to produce the physical response or emotion. Plan what you will do in the scene on your script before you walk into the room. Don't wing it. Have a plan, and be prepared to improvise. Playing actions, and reacting to those that are played by listening and doing, is an integral component to you staying alive as the character. You should treat your script like a score that you are playing and know exactly what emotions and physical actions are necessary to deliver the score.

HOW TO PLAY THE ACTION IN AUDITIONS

Playing the action is another way of approaching the audition with a broader, more expansive exploration of the character. Some say don't play the emotion—play the action—but those two elements are not as distinct as one might think. In simply playing the emotion, an actor may end up playing one note throughout the performance rather than playing multiple notes or riffing off of a phrase within a given composition. For example, if an actor labels a scene "sad" and plays it based on that single emotion, they may miss an opportunity to express a more in-depth understanding of a character and their given circumstances. They may miss opportunities to play subtle shifts in the character's emotional state or articulation of their emotional state through verbal and nonverbal expression.

It's not just what a character feels but what *they do to convey their thoughts and feelings*, conscious and unconscious, that can make the difference in an audition.

So, when preparing for an audition, consider that every character is *doing* something. They may be standing or sitting or walking or jogging or lying down. When you hear acting teachers talk about "playing the action" or "action verbs" and "objectives," this is where those action verbs come in: the verb is the doing. For example, if you are studying when your partner walks into the scene and your first line is, "Oh, hey, honey. I didn't know you were coming home early today," you must play actions that show you are studying and then speak to your partner about their early arrival home. How you do this is based on other clues that you find in the script that tell you the relationship status of the characters. What do you want to accomplish by greeting them in this way? What time of day is it? What are you studying? All of these context clues, including punctuation, in the story impact how you say just one line of your sides. Blowing the line can blow the audition if the selected side drives the storyline.

The sides can only provide limited indication of what a character is doing. Those clues are suggestions made by the writer to indicate how they want the action and transitions of the scene to play out in performance. If you ignore the actions that help convey the character's experiences, you may miss the subtext of what's happening.

Find the actions, use your imagination, and play them. Again, the actions may be in the full script or sides you are provided. You may be asked to invent actions based on context clues. In that case, you need to determine where the character is, who they are with, and what brings them together in order to determine what the character might be doing during the scene or monologue.

Once you identify the set of actions, you should practice them. Props are not typically provided during an audition, so actors sometimes mime props if it serves the scene. For instance, if the actor is on the phone, you might use your own phone as a prop, or your hand, or an imaginary Bluetooth, but doing so should serve the scene and not distract from it. In some cases, it may be more effective to deliver the phone conversation without miming a phone, as though on speaker so that you can be moving around or being still as needed. You should always be thinking about what your character is doing in a given moment so when you play the scene you can be in the moment.

So plan what you will do in the scene on your script before you enter the room. Identify what the character is doing before the scene starts and how that action leads into the scene at hand. For example, maybe the character was jogging and has just entered a scene to find they are being evicted from their apartment and are trying to convince the landlord not to kick them out. In such circumstances, the character may be a bit winded from the jog and might be trying to retrieve items that have been removed from the apartment. Perhaps they are trying to enter the apartment that is being blocked by the landlord. Mark your script to consider at which point the action shifts and the character moves from one moment to the next, and consider why they are moving. To do this, you need to imagine the setup of the space: Where is the apartment door? Where is the landlord in relation to the door? Are there people around? How do you feel about the landlord and the other people? How does that affect your actions?

Again, don't wing it. There is no reason to. You have the right to keep your sides in hand when auditioning. You can break down the action of the scene by imagining the layout (if the details are not provided), identifying the relationships and scenario, and mapping out how you will proceed from the beginning of the scene through the end.

Playing actions and reacting to those that are played are integral components that breathe life into the character. What this means is that if you perform without intention, whether it is movement or stillness, you miss an opportunity to reveal a greater depth of the character and the nature of the relationship in the action and interaction.

Remember, it's not just what a character does but also how they do it. If they sit, it matters if they sit up straight with their back against the chair back with perfect posture as opposed to sitting with the chair backward, straddling the chair while leaning on its back. When and how they choose to rise from the chair is part of the storytelling. You should plot this out before you ever enter the audition room. Map out the terrain of the scene. Where are you in the scene? What were you doing just before, and what will you do after? How does that figure into how you enter and exit? What is the tone of the scene, and how can you convey that in your actions? What do people normally do in these scenarios? How is it similar to or different from usual circumstances? What could you *do* in each

moment of the scene as part of the storytelling, if you had no words
to convey meaning? Let your actions support your understanding of
the words and descriptions you have been provided.

Once you map out the scene using the information provided,
walk through it without using the words. See how you can tell the
story through your actions and interactions. Then return the words
and add the actions, which you will inevitably adjust into a more
fluid presentation. Practice suiting your actions to the words (if the
genre calls for it). But whatever you do, don't wing it. Know what
you're doing, plan what you will do in the room or on tape, and
connect the dots in the story to present a clear and convincing narrative.

PLAYING THE ACTION—JOURNAL PROMPTS

1. Read the sides in their entirety no less than five times. Do not
   make any decisions at first—just read them over and over
   again until you have the story in your body and mind.
2. Mark the story's beginning, middle, and end (or the top three
   key moments in the scene). This can be the full story if you
   have the script or the micro-story represented by the sides.
3. Mark all punctuation in the script. Reflect on what each punctuation mark means in the context of the script, and note how
   it is tied to the action.
4. Identify what the character is *doing* in each line. Look for
   action verbs in the stage and action directions for play, TV,
   and film scripts. You may gain important clues about the
   story by reading what is blocked (or prescribed movement).
5. Read all of the lines, not just your character's lines. Ask
   yourself how your character is communicating how they feel
   from moment to moment and which actions convey this.
6. Review the sides/script for cues of the character, relationship,
   setting, and action.
7. Mark all transitions (these are often called beat changes,
   which are really just shifts in thought, energy, ideas, etc.).

Make specific choices to mark the change, and note which actions shift as a result.

8. Take note of any integral story props (cell phones, cigarettes, etc.) and decide how you are going to use them or mime them in the audition.
9. Connect (or intentionally disconnect) the words your character is saying to the actions you choose, recognizing that different genres and storytelling traditions have distinct needs.
10. Mark your script with exactly how you are going to play the opening and closing actions leading into and out of the scene. You want to leave a strong opening and closing impression. Also, mark a key turning point and related action within the scene to add depth and nuance that can demonstrate your understanding of the story.

The old expression "actions speak louder than words," applies in auditions. So make sure you know what your character is doing when you enter the room. Stay in the story and play every word, thought, and note of punctuation in the script, and you'll increase your callback and booking odds exponentially.

ACTION MAP JOURNAL PROMPTS

Map out your strategy for breaking down your script using this journal prompt to quickly and efficiently break down your scenes:

1. Did you read your script a minimum of five times? Can you tell someone what the story is about in one sentence?
2. Did you consider any racially or ethnically specific references or usages in the script? Describe your character in one sentence.
3. Did you look up any words and punctuation that you didn't know and define them? Write words, definition, and pronunciation, and be sure to practice usage.

4. Did you identify action words to describe what the character is doing at the beginning, middle, and end of the sides? Put action words in order in your journal. Practice the actions in order, mix them up to experiment, and reorder in an effective sequence as part of your audition plan. Be prepared to improvise as needed.

5. Did you read all of the lines, not just your character's lines? Identify key lines that provide information about your character and the relationship with your scene partner.

6. Did you mark all of the emotional transitions on your script? What patterns did you notice? Note what most stands out about your character's emotional state in the selected scene.

7. Did you link your character's actions to your character's story? Note if genre or storytelling traditions call for connecting or disconnecting words and actions.

8. Did you clearly mark the story's beginning, middle, and end? How does the scene flow?

9. Did you mark your script with the opening and closing energy of the scene (e.g., "I'm frustrated at the top. I'm relieved at the end.")? List opening action, turning point action, and closing action as key markers to guide your performance.

10. Did you practice any physical action in your storytelling (e.g., running into the room on the opening line, falling down in a comedic moment, talking on the phone, etc.)? Which felt most in alignment with the scene as written? The least?

11. Did you rehearse and synthesize all of the above so that you have a fluid and thoughtful performance? What did you discover about the character and relationships through the actions?

12. What will you do to help you remember to breathe and own your time in the audition? Document your plan in your journal, and note in the audition whether or not you followed through, not as judgment but as preparation for the next audition. Be sure to reward and encourage yourself.

You are enough. Do the work, and the rest will follow.

6

IDENTIFYING THE EMOTIONS

Every character you play has an emotional landscape. What this means is that every character has a range of emotions connected to their experiences throughout the play, television episode, or film. Your job as the actor is to look for all of the emotional clues that are produced through the action of the play that can be imagined based on what's in the script. The emotional state of the character is sometimes part of the breakdown that describes the character, such as "angry customer," "typical semi-hysterical teenager," and so on. At other times they are dispersed throughout in obvious and less obvious ways.

Sometimes these emotions are tied to stereotypes, which we will discuss in greater detail in chapter 8. Stereotypes are easy "composites" or "sketches" of people that are often used as shortcuts to identify particular archetypes or tropes in human behavior, characteristics, and expectations. Most often, stereotypes are simplistic and do not allow us to get to the depth and breadth of human behavior. In the casting process, there are prevalent aesthetic and behavioral indicators that sometimes help casting directors identify talent for roles on a very basic level. Yet the same indicators can also hinder the casting director by limiting perceptions of what an actor can play based on look rather than skill. Such hindrances limit access to opportunities for actors of the global majority, who may also face uncertainty on how to address the stereotypes when they emerge in relation to emotions during an audition.

How does one go about identifying emotions? Sometimes there are clues hidden in the character breakdown (which many actors ignore and should not—in fact, you should read all of the characters that are connected to yours), the stage directions, or the lines. Look for keywords that describe emotions: angry, sad, frustrated, excited, thoughtful, pensive, and so on (see the emotional vocabulary list at the end of this chapter to help you expand your emotional vocabulary). Once you recognize the emotion words, mark them on your script, wherever they may be. When you recognize the emotional clues in the lines, ask yourself what action you are doing in the scene that produces or expresses the emotion. What punctuation is used that helps the emotion be conveyed in the dialogue? Be sure to also examine the emotional clues in the lines of those characters who are speaking to you or speaking about you.

Sometimes the emotions may be implied in the action rather than directly stated. For example, two characters are having a tense conversation while in the kitchen. One is cooking, while the other enters and begins to speak. The conversation is preceded by parentheticals that indicate mood for the two characters in the scene. One description states, "Her chopping gets louder and faster as he speaks to her." The second description states, "He walks in frustrated." How might you translate these character descriptions into emotional clues that you can play? In this instance, we understand that the person chopping the carrots is a woman. We also learn that she is responding to a man who enters the room, who is described as "frustrated." The way that she cuts the carrots conveys her emotional state, which can be inferred here as perhaps angry, annoyed, busy, or sad. You will not know the character's emotional state from two lines of dialogue, but you can collect clues like these to understand the emotional arc of the character in the scene and/or larger story.

You don't usually have time in any audition to "warm up" or ask questions about motivation, biographies of characters, and so on. You have to be ready to show what is on the page right after your slate. In the case of commercials, you may have only two lines of dialogue, so you have to track and map these emotional states very quickly. Commercial auditions require the actor to present the emotional states very quickly and obviously (think depression medication and lottery commercials), with not much left to the imagination. Similarly, in play, television, and film roles, you have to understand the tone of the piece and the punctuation to know how "big" or "small" you should play the actions to produce the desired emotional outcomes.

In either case, your job as the actor is to read through the script or sides you have been provided and identify the explicit and implicit references to emotions for your character and every character with whom your character interacts throughout the scene. Once you identify the explicit and implicit references, mark them throughout the script.

As we have stated many times before, if you are able to access the full script and know exactly at what point in the story the sides occur, you will have more information to play more levels. In commercial acting, the sides you get are usually the entire script.

TONE AND EMOTION

In network TV and streaming shows, getting the full script will be rare, unless you are an actor in the top 1 percent. However, you can research the director, genre, or creator to identify the style of show you are auditioning for so that you can identify the "tone" of the show. A strong example from television would be *The Handmaid's Tale* (2017) created by Bruce Miller, which has a very specific tone that is icy, dystopic, and reserved in emotional display no matter how intense the emotional state of the character. That tone is very different from a show like Lena Waithe's *Twenties*, which is vibrant and exuberant with emotional displays. Whether an actor of the global majority is called in to "diversify" a show, like the predominantly White *The Handmaid's Tale*, or to provide a larger historically underrepresented racial and ethnic composition, like the predominantly African American *Twenties*,[1] all shows have a tone. The faster you can identify the ways that emotions are performed in relationship to the active doing in the scenes, the closer you get to callbacks and booked jobs.

We like to think of the tone of a show in terms of colors. If you are acting a palette that is primary colors, the performances would be "bright" in color. If you are auditioning for a show that has a more subdued tone (think muted colors varying from shades of white and grayscale to pastels), then playing emotional states in loud, boisterous ways is an ineffective choice in the audition. Be smart about reading the room and doing your research before you get to the job interview (i.e., the audition).

OPENING AND CLOSING OF SCENES

It helps to know the emotional state of the character upon entering the scene, during the scene, and closing the scene. This information will help you identify the emotional arc of the performance (i.e., the shifts in how the character feels over the course of the part of the story you are playing), which may help you avoid playing a flat, one-note performance in the audition.

In order to provide depth and range to your performance, strategically identify how each emotion is linked to the actions expressed by the character. So whether the emotion clue is in the explicit stating of the emotion and you have to translate the emotion into an action, or the clue is in the implicit description of the action and you have to translate that into an emotion, it is important that you recognize both are linked. One does not simply play angry by frowning. A stronger choice is to consider how the character's posture, breathing, facial expression, and tone of voice during a particular action might be influenced by the emotion of anger as well as how anger is culturally expressed, which can vary depending on several factors, including but not limited to gender, religion, race, class, and general circumstances. How I sweep the floor when I am angry compared to when I am inspired may be completely different.

You have to plan exactly what you will do when you go into the room while being prepared to improvise as needed. So, if stage business (i.e., actions that the character is doing or not doing in the scene as they tell the story through dialogue) is not provided in the sides or instructions during the audition, identify some action or present "inaction" (e.g., sitting with purpose, listening intently, staring into space) for your character's performance in the scene. Don't wing it. Planning the physical and emotional score (or map of actions and emotions) will empower you to be present in the mood, state of mind, and given circumstances of the character. The more you know the story you are playing on the page in the moment, the easier the lines will come and the more likely you are to identify an effective choice that can demonstrate your understanding of the character and the material.

You bring the breadth of humanity to the performance when you bring your version of your truth and interpretation of the character. This is what makes you special, so do not try to be anyone but yourself in the room, and let your magic flow, even if it taps into emotion. Stanislavsky-based systems of acting that tell actors to not focus on emotion but to focus on actions, as well as other European-based systems of acting that seek to divorce emotion from acting, may be counterintuitive in some cultures. Global majority approaches to theatrical performance may also separate action from emotion and focus on storytelling (West African griot traditions) or on the actor's body (the Suzuki method) to build an actor's awareness of their body.

As an audition book, we are not advising you to follow any particular method. We believe that you should explore global majority approaches to acting with the same respect and support as you would those that derive from European models, recognizing the variations as central to a range of cultures and traditions that tend to be minimized and ignored or erased in acting programs. Many artists create hybrid technical approaches that source a multinational and cultural collection of acting theories that can enrich your general practice and audition approach.

For new actors, however, the separation between action and emotion can feel very inorganic. Today, we challenge actors of color to think through the cultural contexts that would produce the emotions that they are required to convey on the page in ways that connect to their unique racial, ethnic, and national identities. No matter what the racial identity of the writer or the character written on the page, you can't change who you are in the room, and you don't need to! If you are called in to read for a part that was written for a White or Asian actor and you are Latinx, you may find some cultural discrepancies that make you feel disconnected. The best thing you can do is to be prepared to play exactly what is on the page with as much of you, your humanity, and your talent that you can infuse into the work.

Based on historical and contemporary structure and practice throughout the system of arts and entertainment, many of the plays and shows that you will audition for are not written with actors of the global majority in mind. For the jobs that are advertised as being "for" a person of the global majority, half of those, if not more, are written by a White writer. Lorraine Hansberry, playwright extraordinaire, said, "In order to create something universal, you must pay very great attention to the specific."[2] This is important content for you to consume.

Actions are connected to emotion. This is the missing link in Stanislavsky-based work. The supplement that we offer for playing actions is that you must know what *emotion(s)* the character is feeling in the scene so that you can connect an action that produces or expresses the desired emotion. Be specific!

For example, if your character is mean to another character in the scene and makes them cry, you have to ask, *What action will I play that I can connect to the desired emotional outcome? What will I do with the line that will inspire the emotion?* Will you whisper the line? Will you tease the character with the line? Will you provoke the character with the line? If the direction in the scene says, "Jane is excited as she walks into the room," what action will you play that will produce excitement in you? If you are playing Jane, how will you walk into the room in a way that will show excitement? As the actor, you have to choose an action that will convey the emotion to the casting director. However, if you think backward here, you may discover more actions. If you are in the shoes of the character, what can you do to provoke an emotional reaction like crying? You have to get into the story, not just the character lines, to truly understand the tone of the piece and what actions will incite what emotions within the context of the piece you are auditioning for.

How you focus on actions is important because an action that does not produce an emotional experience is not a great choice. Additionally, attempting to divorce emotions from actions does not align with every culture. Some cultures are highly emotionally expressive in comparison to others. While this has been played in stereotypical ways that undermine the truth of character and circumstances and the humanity of certain cultures, it can be explored in more effective ways in an audition.

August Wilson describes this brilliantly in an interview when he compares a group of Black American men at a diner to a group of Japanese tourists. He describes the ways the Black men joke with one another, argue among themselves, and occupy the space. He distinguishes the Black men from the Japanese men to illustrate the point that a cultural outsider of both groups could easily misread the interactions of either group if they did not understand the culture. While the description could be perceived as stereotypical, the observation of the Black men is grounded in actual interactions observed and experienced by a cultural insider and is evoked to provide a more in-depth representation of Black cultures' impact on intracultural interaction within the context of the United States. [3]

So emotions translate in different ways across cultures. This must be taken into consideration to accurately portray characters from a range of cultures. Keep in mind, the script may not be written with such considerations, for the audition, so you should calibrate your performance according to the script and look for ways to flesh out what is there rather than reinventing it. More of this is discussed in the chapter on sociohistorical context.

You are more likely to succeed in playing a character when recognizing that people feel, and how they express those feelings can vary depending on several factors. Characters are simulations of people, so thus, they have to feel and will convey such feelings through a range of actions or engage in actions that demonstrate their feelings or a selective emotional response that hides their true feelings. Even when a character is not "feeling" anything, they are producing actions that present them as "not feeling" or "trying not to feel," so leave no emotional clue unexplored. Know the character's emotional path and take the casting directors and directors on a journey.

In order to do this, follow this list of steps:

1. Consider your own emotional connection to the story. Though many actors globally use the Stanislavsky-based emotion memory systems, we are not conflating the emotion memory exercises with the emotional identification we are discussing here. There are diverse acting techniques around the world that produce a wide range of approaches that can help actors become skilled craftspeople at the art of acting. From physical theater approaches in England, France, and Japan to sonic and mnemonic approaches to storytelling in Indigenous, Native, African, and South Asian cultures, we urge you not to center or privilege any one acting technique over another, although some approaches may resonate more with your cultural perspectives and goals as an actor (the intercultural list of resources provided in the appendix may offer the information that you need to feel the most empowered on your skill-development journey).

2. Don't deny your feelings about what is happening in the story. If you determine this project is worth pursuing before the audition, trust the story, not just your emotional connections to it. Your life experience may not intersect with the world of the play and the intention of the writer. Equally important is cultural translation. Your cultural experience is shaped by race, class, gender, sexuality, and ability.

3. Though your cultural experiences inform your emotional landscape, don't assume the character you are playing has the same worldview. Trust the words on the page. In other words, understanding the way the character experiences and conveys emotions converges with or diverges from the ways you experience and convey emotions. You may have to practice ways of conveying the emotion through action in ways that do not align with your ways of doing things (e.g., smoking a cigarette under stress when you, yourself, do not smoke). Recognizing the distinctions between the character and you are just as important as recognizing the similarities. It is fine to identify with a character, too, so long as it enhances your ability to portray the character rather than encouraging you to disregard the character as written to simply portray yourself. There may be certain aspects of who you are that shine through in particular moments, but it is important to revisit the script for clues about the character to ensure your interpretation aligns with the creative team producing the show, or at least to provide you with the vocabulary for engaging with them about the performance. In other words, not only may getting too caught up in the character as yourself prevent you from being cast, but also if you are cast and you engage in this and the character's experiences are traumatic and negative, you could be setting yourself up for a troubling experience.

For the audition, if you stick to the clues in the script, understand your instrument and how you can play it to convey emotional state, and know exactly what you are doing in the scene, you will see a more synthesized performance between what you are doing and what you are feeling as the character. The emotional work you do to prepare for the audition is the interior work needed to make the nervous system of your character come to life. If you do this work, you, in turn, will come to life in the room and get closer to booking the job.

EXAMPLES OF EMOTIONAL VOCABULARY

Here is an example of emotional vocabulary that may present itself in the dialogue, stage directions, or action description of your audition sides. Look for these types of words in your storyline so that you can understand the actions and state of mind that your character is experiencing in the world of the play, television, or film for which you are auditioning. Make sure to also look for these types of words in the dialogue of other characters in the sides.

This list will get you started in your journey to identifying emotional clues that reveal what the character is doing and feeling in your scenes. Look for emotion-indicating words, and highlight them in your script. You can break down any number of emotions and find synonyms that allow you to make clever and deliberate choices in your audition. Remember that this list is exemplary, not exhaustive. We encourage you to purchase a synonym dictionary or to use one of the many available online to help you identify the specificity of emotion that you are asked to play in an audition.

- **Anger and Frustration:** Annoyed, Aggressive, Appalled, Apathetic, Affronted, Aggravated, Angry, Antagonized, Arrogant, Belligerent, Bitter, Bristling, Contemptuous, Caustic, Crabby, Cranky, Critical, Cross, Disgusted, Detached, Displeased, Enervated, Exasperated, Frustrated, Furious, Incensed, Indignant, Impatient, Indifferent, Irritated, Miffed, Offended, Peeved, Rattled, Resentful
- **Joy and Happiness:** Amusement, Amusing, Beguiled, Blissful, Blithe, Buoyant, Cheer, Comfort, Cheerful, Delighted, Exuberant, Exalted, Felicitous, Fortuitous, Gladness, Gaiety, Gratification, High-spirited, Hilarious, Jovial, Liveliness, Merry, Mercurial, Rapturous, Rejoicing, Revelry, Regalement, Transported
- **Grief and Sadness:** Affliction, Agony, Anguish, Bereavement, Despair, Desolation, Despondent, Discomfort, Disquiet, Glow, Heartache, Melancholy, Regret, Remorse, Sad, Sorrow, Unhappiness, Woe, Worries, Worrisome, Yearn

- **Fear and Uncertainty:** Anxiety, Angst, Abhorrence, Concentrating, Concerning, Consternation, Dismay, Distress, Despair, Dread, Doubt, Fainthearted, Foreboding, Horrified, Jittery, Scared, Panicky, Suspicious, Uneasy
- **Culturally specific emotional attributes/behaviors:** Bougie, Siddity, Shady, Showing Your Color

IDENTIFYING THE EMOTIONS—JOURNAL PROMPTS

1. As you look at your script or sides, write down all of the emotional clues that you see (directly mentioned in stage directions, in the text, or those implied). Next to each emotion, write down what your character is doing in the scene.
2. Every character you play has an emotional landscape. Write down the emotional state of the character in each scene. Now, write down clues in the character's feelings presented by the playwright or screenwriter (literal or implied) in the text or the breakdown. Once you have them, write them down and make sure everything is justified in the text.
3. Look for contradictions, irony, metaphor, and simile. The character may have stage or action directions such as "angry customer" or "typical semi-hysterical teenager," and so on. At other times, they are dispersed in less obvious ways.
4. Align your emotion identifications with the actions of your character. Write down the actions that produce the emotions you have identified. This will become the map for your script. Remember that you have to bring your unique interpretation based on who you are to the work. Please don't cheat yourself or the casting director out of the opportunity to see who you are and how you interpret the actions and emotional landscape of the story. Synthesizing both action and emotion will help you understand your purpose in the story in the script.
5. Trust your gut. Read the story as many times as you can, and then trust your gut about how the character feels and what

they do. Combine all of these steps, and you will have a clear pathway to guide your performance.

7

UNDERSTAND THE SOCIAL AND CULTURAL CONTEXT CLUES

Social and cultural clues are a part of our everyday lives. We do not have to make them up. Our worldview directly shapes how we decipher these clues. If you are a White female who grew up in a small, all-White rural town in Kansas, you may need support translating the social and cultural context clues about a role that takes place in an urban metropolis where people of all racial, ethnic, gender, class, and ability identities intersect every day. Similarly, if you are African American and are called in to audition for the part of a Nigerian student at Harvard, you may have additional research to complete before the audition. Just because you share a racial or class identification with the character does not mean that you understand their cultural experiences, sociohistorical circumstances, and social position (whether they are upper, middle, lower class, able bodied, disabled, religious, hold tribal affiliations, etc.).

Actors who work consistently are called in based on their "looks" first using the headshot, but secondly they are accessed based on the skills needed to portray the role. Picking up on the cues and deciphering the clues can help you understand what skills are necessary to be believable in the role. For example, if you are auditioning for a play that takes place in 1955 in Alabama and the character you are playing is an African American man in a love scene with a White man, you may simply look at the narrative as portraying an interracial relationship. However, you miss important social and cultural context clues if you do not know the social and cultural composition of life in the southern state of Alabama in 1955. As an actor of color living in the twenty-first century, you have to contextualize the cultural and sociopolitical cues that are in the text. If "Black male, age 22, from Alabama, 1955, in love with White male, age 17" is the casting breakdown, there are social and cultural context clues you can identify for your work right away, before you even get to the dialogue. The first clue would be "Black male, age 22"; ask yourself, *What did it mean to be a Black man in the Southern United States in 1955, when Black people were subjected to horrific social conditions including lynching, police brutality, and sexual assault?*

The second context clue in the breakdown is the same-sex loving relationship. Same-sex and interracial relationships were prohibited in the South at the time and were often punishable by death. For a Black man to be involved in a homosexual, interracial relationship in Alabama in 1955, he would essentially be risking his life. Depending on the rest of the circumstances that are revealed in the actor's dialogue, he could have been forced or consented to the relationship. No matter what the specific relationship of these characters (those are the stakes between the characters in a scene), the sociohistorical facts surrounding the time period should tell the actor that no matter what the dialogue, there is a great risk for the Black character in the relationship whether or not it was a loving one.

Using a twenty-first-century worldview to play a mid-twentieth-century homosexual relationship reveals a lack of preparation on the part of the actor to the casting director.

Other sociohistorical context clues that could help you as an actor contextualize the relationship in 1955 include Emmitt Till's brutal lynching at the hands of White men for supposedly whistling at a White woman and Rosa Parks's arrest for not giving up her seat on a Montgomery, Alabama, bus, which launched the Montgomery bus boycott to end segregation in the South. The United States' involvement in the Vietnam War (the Second Indochina War) officially began on November 1, 1955, with the arrival of the U.S. Military Assistance Advisory Group in South Vietnam. So, besides the fact that an interracial gay couple would be completely shocking in that time period, the international social climate was fraught with racial and political tensions. These are just examples of cursory clues and assessments that you can make based on a breakdown of the script.

What's important overall is for you to make certain that you (1) do your research and make sure you understand the context of your amazing body as a person with intersecting identities that are always in conversation with any text you play, from Shakespeare to the most contemporary avant-garde performance; and (2) resist imposing your worldview onto an experience or time period. Your personal social, cultural, and political standpoints may have everything or nothing to do with the position of your character. However, your body and its racial identification within particular social, historical, and political contexts is something that you cannot change and must accept wholly as you approach the work. Think of your instrument as a vital medium for the storytelling. In order to do so, understand how your body will be read and how it will contribute to the story, rather than pretending that how you appear as the character will not be a factor. Don't try to be what "they" (i.e., casting directors) want you to be. Be the actor who owns who they are and does the work needed to play what is on the page in the most truthful and prepared way possible.

The structural racism and ableism of the entertainment industry at large throughout history has residual manifestations in the casting and directing processes that actors experience daily in the twenty-first century. The entertainment industry and actor training programs that are centered in Eurocentric norms attempt to erase race, culture, sexuality, ability, and religion from the casting process as an important consideration for actors. Roles that are written by and for Black, Latinx, Indigenous, Pacific Islander, Asian, Middle Eastern, North African, or any other historically marginalized and excluded racial or ethnic group still run the risk of trafficking in stereotypes, which we will cover in the next chapter. However, your race, culture, and experiences are valuable and should be affirmed in- and outside the work.

We cannot and should not wait for casting directors to tell us we are worthy of great stories, characters, opportunities; we have to tell ourselves. When facets of our identities are too often used to diversify (i.e., decorate) the normative Whiteness of a project that we audition for, it can trigger us to feel angry and upset. But think about this. You have the power to choose what you want to do in this life. If you do not like how a project portrays your racial or ethnic group or any racial or ethnic group, you can make the choice on how to proceed. The producers and directors of the project can claim that they are "inclusive" and "diverse" as much as they like, but it is up to us to decide when and how we participate in work that devalues our identities. Seeking out and creating projects that align with our values is a viable option, however challenging.

As an actor, be aware of the systems of inequality that exist in our business and try to avoid assimilating your bodies, voices, and views to fit these so-called standards to avoid long-standing trauma that can affect your quality of life by developing a healthy process of identifying roles and preparing auditions in advance. No role is worth your mental wellness and dignity. Many characters written as generic "people of color" or "Black," Asian," "Latinx," and so on, are written for a White gaze due to the historical lack of PGM writers, directors, and producers writing characters of non-White descent in positions of power throughout the entertainment industry.

Actors internalize many of these systemic ideologies and, thus, try to change themselves in order to fit into the cookie-cutter descriptions and ideas of the entertainment industry. As an artist who is working to strengthen your technical abilities in a craft and entertainment system that systematically works to undervalue your experiences and your labor, you must find a sustainable and healthy way to pursue work in this industry without submitting your body to physical, psychic, and emotional damage.

You are worthy, and your talent is yours. The systemic racial inequity embedded in the training and professional acting field does not define you. Contrary to popular belief, you are not "lucky" to get an audition or opportunity. You can choose what you want to audition for and what roles you want to play. When you feel as if a role is written to disparage or denigrate your racial, ethnic, gender, and/or class position, you can choose to turn it down before you even audition. Seek out other opportunities, and create your own work. If you choose to go, stand strong and make choices that are informed by your research of the social, historical, and cultural circumstances of the script and your knowledge of stereotypes so that you can actively subvert them.

People of the global majority have lived through trials and tribulations as much as successes across time and history. Knowing your history helps, so learn as much as you can about your personal and cultural background. When you know who you are and how your body is read when you enter the audition room, you can honor the dignity you find within roles that position PGM as "less than" and that rely on negative stereotypes of people of color. Actors from various cultural backgrounds have achieved this in spite of the limitations imposed by the industry. We do not have to be reduced to the stereotypes of our diverse cultural experiences imposed on us by oppressive structures, even though this is an ongoing resistance struggle.

For example, in the history of African Americans in theater, film, and television in the United States, Black people have been depicted as slaves, minstrels, maids, concubines, pimps, prostitutes, and a host of other racial stereotypes. These roles were written to degrade and marginalize Black people within the power hierarchy of the Black/White binary in the United States. However, in playing these roles and recognizing the necessity of representing the range and depth of our humanity through storytelling, many Black actors have given performances that spoke to their spirit of resilience and endurance to subvert major stereotypes. They have played these roles with strength and dignity, thus honoring the experiences of servitude that many Black people before them experienced in everyday life and in the entertainment industry.

Make sure you are identifying strong boundaries between your beliefs and the beliefs and experiences of your character. When you are auditioning for a character who has sensibilities similar to yours, that's a wonderful thing. However, you must make certain that the perspectives that you think you share do not cloud your judgment and trigger emotional outcomes in the audition that you don't plan for when preparing your audition material. Again, this can lead you to play your personality rather than the part as it is written. It can also lead to challenges if you book the role and are unprepared or ill-equipped to make the distinction, especially in potentially traumatic roles.

Many Stanislavsky-based acting practices suggest that you substitute a lived experience to perform a particular emotion for a character. Likewise, non-Stanislavsky-based or supplemental Stanislavsky-based acting systems such as Jazz Acting and Theatrical Jazz acting, the Black Arts Institute, the Hendricks Method, Susan Batson Studio, Culture Clash, Black and Latinx Improv, Black Theatre, Womanist Truth Work, Hip-Hop Theatre, and other approaches are acting systems that you can investigate that can help you strengthen or maintain your acting practices. Identify and explore the approaches that allow you to present your best and most affirmed self in the audition room.

Remember, each audition is a job interview. If you experience emotional triggers at a job interview, you have to be able to demonstrate some sense of self-regulation as the trigger takes hold; otherwise, you risk potentially appearing ill equipped to manage your emotions in a professional manner.

Acting approaches that ignore the diversity of students and the different ways they may see the world and learn from it in the acting classroom can have an adverse effect on the actor. We have heard many actors say things such as "I'm not political" or "I'm not an [insert ethnicity] actor: I am an actor that happens to be [insert ethnicity]," or "I want to play universal roles." We ask this question in return: Who gets to represent the universal? How do we know?

Any actor, regardless of race, culture, or additional, intersecting identities can and should be able to represent the universal. Unfortunately, the system has historically operated to thwart culturally diverse portrayals as universal experiences even though everyone's experiences have the right to be read as "universal." While we believe the system can and will change through collective efforts, it is still a work in progress. Therefore, we want you to be brave and take up space with confidence and assurance that your specific worldview allows you to understand a script. The great thing is that, even if you do not initially understand, you can do the work and prepare to go into the room equipped to succeed in the interview and make it to the next round: the callback.

CALLBACKS

Callbacks occur when the impression you leave with the casting director tells them that you have what it takes to play the part on the page as the writer and director imagine it. When you are called back, your job is to convince the casting director that what they saw in the first round was not a fluke and that your take on the character is clearly crafted. It is generally a good idea to wear the same clothing to the callback to help casting directors identify you more easily.

The social and cultural context clues that you find help you defend your choices when you go to the callback. In callbacks, you may have to talk to the writer, director, and producer in addition to the casting director. Knowing the reasons *why* you made the choices that you did should come from the text and your research of the text, not something that you make up or assume.

Do exactly what you did at the first audition, but be prepared to take direction from the casting director or to improvise when asked to do so. This is why we tell you to keep reading the sides over and over—so that the story comes naturally for you. If you are asked to improvise "as the character," on camera in the callback, you should have enough information based on your research as context clues to perform as if you are the character in that moment.

As a twenty-first-century actor, you have particular social and cultural cadences, physical gestures, and experiences that are historically situated in the now and that cannot be transferred across time periods. The ways you move, speak, gesture, and interact are very specific to the culture and body in which you live. One can see from archival footage of the late nineteenth and early twentieth centuries that there is a distinct difference between the gait of people then and now. If you look at videos of plays, TV shows, and films from the late twentieth through the early twenty-first centuries, much has changed with how people interact as well. Time is time, and you have to pay attention to how it shapes behavior when you are acting and reacting in a scene. Equally important are the various oppressions and limitations projected onto particular bodies in varying moments in time.

The internet gives you a wealth of research resources at your fingertips, from YouTube videos to sources at the Library of Congress. By simply watching films from different eras, or interviews of people speaking with various accents and dialects, you can discover volumes about the times in which those people existed. Many things contribute to how they walk: age, gender, race, and culture, as well as attire, cultural background, and more. All of these factors must be taken into consideration when preparing for an audition.

When it comes to gender identifications, your self-identification and the identification of your character may intersect, or they may be very far from one another socially, culturally, or politically. Researching cisgender identifications of the past may be a great deal easier than nonbinary identities simply because many nonbinary subjects in history may have hidden their gender fluidity for fear of persecution. Films and television shows such as *The Danish Girl* (2015), *Transamerica* (2005), *All About My Mother* (1999), *Boys Don't Cry* (1999), *Tangerine* (2015), *Paris Is Burning* (1990), *Pose* (2018 to present), and many others have opened opportunities for actors to explore the ways that both cisgender and nonbinary actors have portrayed nonbinary and nonheteronormative identifications. You must keep in mind that, similar to White actors playing in blackface in the late nineteenth through the mid-twentieth centuries, so too have cisgender actors attempted to play trans, queer, or non-binary characters and able-bodied actors portraying disabilities in offensive depictions.

We encourage you to make informed decisions when deciding to play outside of your racial, ethnic, or gender identification, due to the oppressive history of cross-racial and cross-gender performance in theater, film, and television. We cannot tell you what to do, but we can make you aware of the racial, gender, and ableist transgressions that exist in performance history around the world.

Many actors of color think that racial transgression is impossible if you are a part of a racially oppressed group. This is not the case. Racial transgression and cultural appropriation can occur between racial groups and do not have to happen between dominant and oppressed groups and people of the global majority. Racial transgressions and cultural appropriation can occur between racial groups with a history of oppression. We encourage you to stand in solidarity with all racially oppressed groups and to protect one another when offered the opportunity to advance by oppressing another racial, ethnic, or gender identity.

All in all, the actor must be thorough in their investigation of the culture, historical moment, and social mores of the time in order to add significant layers to an audition and ultimately to the performance. Falling back on gender, racial, and ableist stereotypes not only is a superficial approach but also can lead to errors that limit the specificity of your audition and can cost you your job.

Ultimately, the hard part of auditioning is that you usually do not have time to do that much work before your audition date. In most cases, you find out you have a potential call two to three days before the audition. This is why it is helpful to read and prepare generally as part of your daily practice. Try to learn something new each day that could directly or indirectly relate to roles you might play. You never know when such information will come in handy.

If you are submitting your audition online via self-tape, you really have to make quick decisions and turn around the self-tape (or video of you performing the sides) quickly to the agent or casting director. This is why you must synthesize your audition process and script breakdown steps so that you can get to the job of acting.

HISTORICAL AND CULTURAL CONTEXT CLUES: JOURNAL PROMPT LIST

Here are six steps that can help you quickly summarize what we have discussed about historical and cultural context clues so that you can show the casting director that you understand the framing of the role in your performance. List your answers to the questions below in your journal.

1. Make sure you list all dates or references in the script that connect you to time periods, such as books, music, films, and so on, that are named by the writer. Do you have these?
2. Did you list any references to race, ethnicity, gender, sexuality, or ability mentioned in stage directions, character dialogue, and action descriptions? Note these references and look them up to make sure you know what they mean and how they pertain to the story and its tone.
3. Did you ask yourself how your racial, ethnic, sexuality, class, ability, or gender identification can help you understand the clues in the story, if at all?
4. Write down how you synthesize the sociohistorical and cultural framework of the world of the story.
5. If you are in a period piece, did you note how you might adjust voice, physicality, and interactions accordingly? If you should have an accent, add it in. If your physical gestures indicate the time period, incorporate them. Map all of the clues and link them together. Remember, any time period that is not your current one can be understood as a period piece.
6. Did you leave room to think the thoughts of the character through your pursuit of the actions and the emotional clues? Casting directors do not want to see all of your "actor" work; they want the end result, which is an excellent performance.

8

FACE STEREOTYPES

Now that you have explored how to identify the historical and cultural context clues in a script, we want you to think about facing stereotypes. Stereotypes come in many forms, from racial and ethnic stereotypes that reveal power dynamics between racial and ethnic groups, to gender, class, ability, and sexual identification stereotypes that attempt to belittle and marginalize particular identifications or even refuse to acknowledge their humanity.

As we have discussed, actors of the global majority often have to read for roles that were written by writers who are not people of color. You may be asked to perform stereotypes of your racial, ethnic, or cultural identity in ways that are demeaning. By this we mean you will be asked to be more "Black," "Asian," "Latinx," and so on, according to expectations set by precedents that cater to White supremacist assumptions about people of the global majority. These are microaggressions that must be addressed so that you can do your work. But how do you address them? If you book a commercial or play that traffics in racial, ethnic, or gender stereotypes, how do you reconcile the problematic perceptions?

In most instances, you make the decision to perform stereotypes as soon as you accept an audition where the writing reveals these representations. You give consent to the casting director that you are willing to play the role by showing up for the audition. You have a couple of options before that step that can help you with your decision. The first person you can address is your agent or manager, if you have one. Before you agree to take an audition that appears possibly degrading because of the stereotypes or occupation of a particular character of color, ask your agent what the casting director expressed when soliciting you for the call. If your agent confirms what you sense in reading the script or the sides, you must decide at that moment, before you go on the call, if you want to take the role.

Actors are "typed" because writers have particular characters in mind that serve a particular role in delivering the story to the audience. Over time, we have been able to categorize these types as integral to storytelling. The female ingénue, the leading man, the best friend, and so on. When these types are racialized as other than "White," the historic ghosts of racial stereotypes enter the room before you show up, no matter who is writing. Having a strong idea of your personal boundaries, as we discussed earlier, and what type is being called to the audition is crucial in helping you identify what you need to do before you accept or decline that audition, as well as in the casting room. We are not judging actors who decide to take auditions that portray stereotypes. We simply want to acknowledge that these roles may feel triggering for actors in ways that they cannot imagine during the audition, callback, or final booking.

How does casting work in relation to stereotypes?[1] The casting director works with agents by soliciting submissions from their pool of talent who fit the speculations of the breakdown. What you list on your résumé and what you look like are the principal reasons why you are called for the job interview.

Calls for people of color in the industry breakdowns, even for predominantly Black, Asian, or Latinx shows, are usually very specific and often use racial stereotypes in the descriptions of the characters. For example, a breakdown asking for an Asian American actor who is a "super smart math whiz" uses racial stereotypes of Asian Americans as being good at math, part of the "model minority myth" that is used in mainstream media. Similarly, a casting breakdown calling for an African American man who is a "thug type" or "hip-hop guy" reeks of hypermasculine Black male stereotypes.

So what do you do when you are confronted with these generalized and often-demeaning descriptions? One tactic is to call your agent for more information about the script. Is there a shift in the narrative where stereotypes are subverted? Is the project a satire? If you do not receive a favorable answer to your question, perhaps you will decide to pass on the role. If you do not have an agent, you can research the past work of the writer or director to investigate what type of work they do. If you find a trail of similar stereotype trafficking, maybe this is not the project for you. If you have no emotional triggers in playing stereotypes and really just want to make the money and take the opportunity, that is your choice. In both instances, you need to plan before the audition.

It makes no sense to go on an audition for the part of a stereotype if you know that you will not take the job.

Many famous actors have played stereotypes and have found a way to bring dignity to those roles. Halle Berry and Samuel L. Jackson played people with a crack cocaine addiction in Spike Lee's *Jungle Fever* (1991) to great critical acclaim. Many screenwriters and directors across racial lines have used racial stereotypes to make particular social and political points. Other writers and directors simply traffic in stereotypes for capital gains. Many actors have played stereotypical roles and made great opportunities out of the work.

The bottom line is that the entertainment industry is a predominantly White, male, heteronormative space that controls most of the opportunities for the top 1 percent of actors who work full time in theater, film, and television. That said, using the audition time to voice concerns over the content will not make a difference and will only label you as "difficult" to work with for future auditions. By doing your homework before you agree to the audition, you can make a quick assessment of the material and decide very quickly if auditioning and booking the job can help you reach your career goals. This does not mean you can't decline unsafe situations (see chapter 1 on boundaries and wellness).

SUBVERT THE STEREOTYPES

Every role depicting a person of color is connected to racial, ethnic, and gender stereotypes to some degree. This is due to the fact that so much of the writing for American and European theater, film, and television has historically been dominated by White men. (Women from all backgrounds and people of the global majority have always taken part in creating their own works that have received less attention and resources.) These stereotypes are written in conscious and subconscious acts that can traumatize, silence, undermine, and injure people of the global majority. Such stereotypes may be apparent in the character description, which may use adjectives and adverbs to describe a character in a way that overtly or covertly stereotypes a particular group, either intentionally or unintentionally.

This is why it is important to read the story and not just the lines, as discussed in chapter 3. You must know the genre to help determine if the stereotyping is a part of the storytelling or rather how it is integrated into the storytelling in ways that reinforce or contradict the stereotype. Either way, we suggest that you face these stereotypes head-on and ask specific questions of your social, cultural, and political standpoints. The more familiar you are with the entire story and contexts, the better equipped you will be to raise such questions and incorporate resistance strategies as needed should you eventually be offered the role and decide to accept it.

While this book is written in the context of people of the global majority in the United States, racial and ethnic stereotypes are part of the social construct of race and are used to identify power structures throughout the world—albeit in distinct, national contexts. Therefore, the actor should take into consideration the national context of the story along with the various other factors discussed in chapter 7 in relation to the social, historical, and cultural contexts in order to identify and potentially disrupt stereotypes through performance.

When writers of the global majority create plays, television, film, and streaming projects, they may be offering counter-narratives to existing stereotypes that attempt to further marginalize historically underrepresented groups in the United States and abroad. They may also be part of reinscribing these stereotypes. Internalized racism and sexism are so deeply embedded in the American and European entertainment outlets that dominate the industry and the formal training processes at predominantly White universities and acting studios where most actors train that distinguishing who is and isn't writing stereotypes is not really the point here. There is no guarantee that the author who is a cultural insider will avoid the historical stereotyping that has become so entrenched in storytelling across platforms, as they are at times coerced into trafficking in stereotypes in order to gain access. So take nothing for granted. Be prepared to mine any script you receive for the social, historical, and cultural contexts, regardless of who is writing, and also identify and combat stereotypes to the best of your ability should you choose to subvert them.

If you choose to play roles that traffic in stereotypes because they are part of a sociohistorical moment where people of the global majority are politically, culturally, and socially marginalized, then you have to find agency and dignity in playing these roles. Taking the time to create your historical and cultural context map of the script, guided by chapter 7, can help you flesh out many of the stereotypes or, more specifically, implied or explicitly racial, ethnic, and/or gender references. As you search for stereotypes, consider the genre and note that certain theatrical genres over time, such as melodramas, period pieces, horror, and experimental pieces, have historically included stereotypes as part of the formulaic structure. In this instance, try to determine if the stereotype presented in the character description, dialogue, stage directions, and design elements (set, costume, sound, etc.) are written to reinforce or challenge the stereotype. Familiarize yourself with the stereotype so that you can identify clues in the writing that pertain to voice, physicality, emotional expression, and interactions that will help you understand how to manipulate your performance.

IDENTIFYING AND SUBVERTING STEREOTYPES

Key things that you can look for in the script that can help you identify stereotypes and their potential subversions include:

1. **Accents and dialects:** Does the character speak the primary language of the play? Do they speak with an accent? Is the accent regional or ethnic or both? It is important to get very specific in this regard. If a character is described as having a "Hispanic" accent, what does that mean? There is no generic "Hispanic" accent, so ask questions of the text. Is it an accent originating from a South American nation or the Caribbean? Is the character first generation, second generation, or third? What race is the character? It is possible to be "Hispanic" or "Latinx" and also be Black, Indigenous, and so on. Consider these details as you review the dialogue in the script to identify how the character uses language.

2. **Rewrite the lines:** Once you identify any words that seem to indicate an accent or dialect, rewrite the lines in a way that is more clear to you. Once you know what the character is saying in the way that you speak, you can find the pacing and intonations in the accent or dialect more easily. Also, see chapter 4 on punctuation and pronunciation for more suggestions.

3. **Use your script:** Use the script as your foundation. Everything the character says leads back to the bigger story. Understand that your role is part of the whole and cannot stand without the other parts. Both stereotypes and seemingly "authentic" characters of color written in the script are part of the narrative structure.

4. **Identify physicality:** Look for descriptions about the physicality of the character to see if anything indicates stereotypes. For example, if a character is described as someone "who has a hip-hop swagger" or "a fiery Latin spirit," these descriptions are rooted in longstanding stereotypes that have lingered in the White American imagination and Eurocentric dramatic

works and performance traditions. Start with the character breakdown to scan for implicit or explicit racist, sexist, homophobic, ableist, or xenophobic stereotyping in physicality. If it is there, see if you can split the difference (to give them a bit of what they expect and more of what you know about the humanity of such a character) to play the character in a way that makes you feel empowered.

5. **Synthesize emotional descriptions and actions:** Make sure any emotional "displays'" in your performance are not stereotypical or superficial, but are thoughtful engagements with what the character needs or wants in the scene. Your job is to stay in the story by playing exactly what is on the page, one line and one action at a time. Identify any emotions associated with your character in the character breakdown, dialogue, and stage directions that can be connected to stereotypes, such as speech, physical gestures, costuming, or other elements. You want to map these opportunities in advance of your audition so that you can mine them for their potential during the performance.

In sum, none of these character discoveries, in terms of voice, physicality, or emotional expression, can be divorced from considerations of relationships. This is why it is critical that you know who your character is speaking to or interacting with at all times and understand how the social, historical, and cultural contexts factor into their relationship to stereotypes or their subversions by writers and directors. Again, considering the historical patterns of particular genres and relationships, racial and sexist stereotyping can be embedded in a piece regardless of the intention of the author. Your job is to interpret the character as it is written, which may require some adapting, using the script as a point of departure, rather than creating something completely new from scratch. In some instances, you make a choice to play a racially stereotypical character as a stereotype without adaptation, and thus portray a demeaning character for money. For example, in the early 2000s Mary J. Blige filmed a Burger King commercial where she sang a song about loving fried chicken. This imagery reinforced longstanding racial stereotypes about African Americans loving to eat chicken. After many incensed customers and fans of Blige's music protested her reinforcement of stereotypes by threatening to boycott the Burger King franchise, the commercial was pulled from circulation.

Previous generations had fewer choices and opportunities yet still devised strategies that dignified their choices. From Hattie McDaniel's performance of a maid in *Gone with the Wind* (1939) when few if any upstanding roles were available to African Americans, to Rita Moreno's exuberant, Oscar-winning representation in *West Side Story* (1961), or Morgan Freeman's dignified and subversive performance of a hired driver in *Driving Miss Daisy* (1989), actors of color have made choices to advance their careers. For many actors, stereotypical portrayals and subversions have, and will continue to be, part of the consideration process.

Representations of gender and sexual identifications in the intersecting LGBTQIA+ members of the global majority can also be offensive and demeaning. Watching and listening to gender- and queerphobic language in theater, film, and television shows is par for the course in entertainment; however, the social justice activism of many artists has made space for artists to insist on representation that amplifies and empowers diverse racial, ethnic, gender, and sexual identifications. We have a long way to go to feel safe and secure on our stages and screens as people of the global majority, but we do have greater interracial and intraracial awareness that has enabled artists to speak up and out when they experience or witness injustices on sets and stages around the world.

You make the choice to reject or accept these roles when you see the sides for your audition. It is true that some roles can be more easily adapted to disrupt racial and sexist stereotypes than others. It is a risk either way. This is why it is important to read the script beforehand, analyze the clues, and map a strategy for preparing and producing the performance in the audition. If you find through the initial reading or preparation process that there is no effective way for you to use your instrument to disrupt the racial or sexist stereotype, pass on the role before wasting your time or the casting director's time. There may be other actors who find a way to achieve the goal or are willing to play the stereotype for money. This is why establishing your boundaries and having a wellness plan is key to your success and well-being.

You have the agency to decide what types of roles you want to play, regardless of industry tropes that you have to "take what you can get." There are a range of possibilities for accessing roles and types of work that do not traffic in stereotypes, as well as the possibility of creating your own projects. You are in charge of the path you take and the work you do. Own your process, and take control of all of the elements that you can. Luck is when opportunity meets preparation, so how prepared will you be? In the next chapter, we talk about synthesizing all of these steps in the breakdown to create a successful self-tape, which is increasingly becoming the number 1 way that actors audition.

STEREOTYPES AND COUNTER-NARRATIVES

The following journal prompts can help you identify stereotypes so that you can identify ways to counter offensive depictions of diverse racial, ethnic, gender, abilities, and sexual identifications that might present themselves in your scripts. We cannot tell you how to act, but we can help you face the dualities actors of the global majority face working within and around the racist structures that are at the foundation of the entertainment industry. We want you to feel empowered by your boundaries and how you maintain them within society.

FACE STEREOTYPES—JOURNAL PROMPTS

1. **Listen to your gut:** Do any lines in your script make you feel uncomfortable in the way the characters talk to or about one another as it pertains to race, ethnicity, gender, ability, or sexuality? Write these down.

2. **Note the time period/time of day or evening:** Do the scenes in your script take place in the past, present, or future? Once you know this, write down how any stereotypes or surface descriptions of people of the global majority, LGBTQIA+, or people with variable abilities might be perceived during the time period of the piece. *Note*: Period pieces are not uniquely works that happened "a long, long time ago." A period piece can also take place within ten years of the current moment.

3. **Look for stereotypical descriptions and language:** Write down what you know about the stereotypical or negative language that you encounter on the page. Do you see anything that can help you connect to the pretext and context of the story?

4. **Pay attention to language usage:** Are you familiar with the language usage, character description, physicality, vernacular, and so on, of your character? Is the character's speech casual? Formal? Slang? Write down the how and why for your character's use of language. Be specific in your language usage, and look up every word and pronunciation that you don't know.

5. **Do your homework:** Have you done all of your homework to historically situate your character within the world of the play, TV show, film, or television commercial you are auditioning for?

6. **Mind your boundaries:** Is playing this character within the scope of your personal boundaries? How do these stereotypes or descriptions reinforce or challenge what you know about the character from the text? If you feel uncomfortable, write that down and make a decision about how you want to proceed. No job is worth losing your personal compass of right and wrong.

9

SELF-TAPES

There used to be a time when actors actually showed up for auditions in person. Since March 2020, the world has been engaged in a global pandemic and international protests against anti-Black violence by police and systemic inequality in the entertainment industry. But the self-tape trend began long before these converging pandemics.

According to statistics posted on SAG-AFTRA's website in September 2019, "Self-taping accounts for roughly 85% of all auditions, and that percentage is only going to increase."[1] Actors had acclimated to self-taping in their homes and apartments for many years before COVID-19 and international quarantines and social justice protests. However, in light of these social and cultural circumstances, actors of the global majority are at a crossroads of change, as the entertainment industry must look at itself in the wake of Black Lives Matter demands that challenge systemic inequality and racism in entertainment.

For the most part, there are more jobs than there are working actors, between regional theater and major markets like Los Angeles, New York, Atlanta, and Chicago as well as television, film, streaming, and commercial opportunities. As diversity is "trending" in entertainment, we must work together to draw the industry's attention to demands for equity and inclusion as well as the recogni-

tion of affinity markets in creative projects that speak to the multiracial history of American and European modernity in the twenty-first
century. We all need to get comfortable with the possibility that
from our kitchen, studies, and bedroom, opportunities to present
ourselves for roles across the platforms are alive and well.

The information we have provided here will serve as a self-tape
primer to help you organize your self-tape studio at home. Using
our breakdown method will make the steps toward synthesis and
preparedness for your auditions easier. The technical part is easy.
Here, we help you shape and design your audition for in-person or
self-tape presentation.

PREPARING THE AUDITION

Self-tapes provide an extra layer of concern for many actors because
the technology itself can be expensive, which makes creating a self-
tape difficult for artists who don't have the financial resources to
prepare their work. Many actors cannot afford fancy backgrounds or
cameras, lights, and editing software. How can they compete with
the many non-union and SAG-AFTRA members who not only have
better training, but also have self-tape studios that rival professional
casting offices? Something you need to consider, besides all of the
work to identify the clues and cues in your script, is the technical
component of self-taping.

TECHNICAL EQUIPMENT

In your wildest imagination, you would have custom backgrounds, a
great camera, a lighting and wardrobe designer, an editor and color-
correction person, technical direction, costumes and props, slates
and reels, and adept readers who could help you shine in your audition. But who can afford all of these things? After researching the
advice of a multiracial cohort of casting directors from coastal,
southern, and mid-markets[2] we are able to offer the following tips to

help you develop a cost-efficient self-tape studio at home as well as quality self-tapes that reflect all of the amazing work you have done to prepare the role before you.

Often actors are so worried about how they look that they lose track of the story and the reason they are auditioning. One peeve of casting directors is actors who send distracted and poorly crafted self-tapes that do not focus on the work but instead look like an indie film, with flashy credits and weird angles that distract from the actor's performance. Instead of focusing on their lines and telling the story of the character, the actors deliver distracting self-tapes that don't do the script or their talent any justice. The following insider tips will help you craft a basic setup to present yourself through various self-submission outlets until you find an agent or manager who will submit on your behalf. Even when you do identify and secure an agent, you will still be asked to send in self-tapes and voice-over reels for the audition. So, to paraphrase Tiffany Haddish, "Be ready."

TECHNICAL TIPS

You can spend a lot of money buying expensive equipment, or you can just use what you have and present the best work possible. The first thing you should consider is your background. You should choose a solid background that you can place on a wall using adhesives or tape. The edges should be symmetrical and out of the frame. Think about the backgrounds for your elementary and middle school photos that were gray, brown, or pale blue. You need to replicate those backgrounds. Don't choose a background that is distracting with patterns. Wear clothing that pops away from the background. Avoid matching your clothing to the background.

Invest in a small tripod with a remote control that will let you click "Play" from the mark where you set up your camera. Using your mobile phone as the camera, make sure that you mark your sight lines off to the side of the phone (use a Post-it or other marker) so that you have a point of connection for the reading. Some folks

cut paper "eyes'" from magazines to look into during their performance.

In the best-case scenario, you will have someone who can read
live with you. If you cannot find anyone to read with you, try an
acting app that will read the scene with you. Another way that you
can create a reading partner is to record the lines of the character
that you are in conversation with and leave space in between for
your character's lines. You have to make the best out of what you
have so that you can get the best product. Your background should
be clear of distractions, and your space should be silent—no children talking in the background, no dogs, no books, no movie pos-
ters, and so on, just a solid one-color background and a camera set
up for a shoulder and headshot delivery of the monologue or scene.

LIGHTING

It is important that your best look and performance are presented in
your self-tape. If you look like you are lost in an alley or an under-
ground tunnel, nine times out of ten the casting director will move
on from your tape. Invest in an inexpensive halo lamp or another
soft light that will illuminate you so that the picture is very clear for
the audition. Amazon has a series of inexpensive ring lights that
include small camera rigs and remote-control access.

If you cannot afford to buy a tripod, prop your phone against
something level so that you can get a clear sight line in your tape.
Do a few test shots to make sure that the angles are straightforward
with the lighting and the sound is crisp and clear.

PLAYING THE SCENE

So many actors are worried about being "off book" on an audition;
however, many are so focused on the lines and not the story that
they lose the train of thought of their character. You have to trust
that a casting director called you after seeing your headshot and

résumé because they actually hope that you are a match for the part. You can use your sides in the audition, but not as a crutch. You have to make sure that the focus of your performance is the camera. If you have someone read with you, make sure that they are positioned near your sight line so that your eyes are not moving all over the place as you follow the script. Use your finger to track the first line of the dialogue, or monologue, and continue to track down the scene as the reader reads with you. Make certain that your opening and closing lines are clear and visible to the camera. Do not keep looking down at your script. Lift your paper up to chest level and look as much as you can to the camera side line.

PUNCTUATION AND PRONUNCIATION RULES

Remember our chapter on punctuation? Minding the punctuation and pronunciation is important for your self-tape because playing it correctly conveys to the casting director that you understand the tone and tempo of the scene. Do not be afraid to ask questions of your agent or the casting director before you start your performance. In the case of self-tapes, ask your agent or manager (or email the casting director if you are self-submitting through a casting service as an independent) for assistance. Try to exude as much confidence in your abilities as you can through your performance. Memorize as much as you can, but keep your script in hand just in case you need to "grab" a line or are thrown off by the way the reader recites a line or responds to something you said in character. Don't forget: if at first you don't succeed, try, try again. Take advantage of the retake and erase and start anew, if needed. Once you run the tape a few times, your errors will be clear to you so you can edit and redo it as needed. Do your best to make your audition perfect.

SELF-TAPE LABELS AND EDITS

You can label and edit your self-tape using Adobe, iMovie, Magisto, or any number of free editing software options. Just make sure that you leave your slate until after you drop into the audition. You can use your slate (see the "Slates" section below) as the "tag" for the audition. If you do not get your audition out, on, and engaged ASAP, most likely casting directors who don't love your slate will turn your tape off and never see your audition.

SOUND

Make sure that you check your sound levels before you submit your tape. If you are singing, make the adjustment for the close proximity of the microphone on your phone. If you are acting, make sure that you are following the speech patterns and levels of the character while adjusting as the actor to fit your performance within the frame of your phone camera. Follow the rules for enunciation and clarity. If your role requires an accent or dialect, don't sacrifice meaning and clarity by overdoing it. Remember, casting directors look at hundreds of self-tapes a week. The last thing they want to see is an audition that is dark and poorly edited and an actor who is not off-book, always looking down, dropping lines, and sometimes creating. They deserve better than that, and so do you. Try to eliminate all background noise and distractions so that the casting director can focus on your amazing performance and not the faults in the production.

SLATES

Slates are introductory videos that you use to say who you are and what agency you are with before an audition. Your slate is your introduction to the camera. Make sure that you film your slates and self-tapes in *landscape* mode (horizontal), not portrait (vertical).

Your slate should contain your name, agency, the role you're auditioning for, and face shots, both front and profile. In some instances, casting directors won't ask you for profiles, but just expect it anyway. If you do not have an agent, you can identify as "independent." Make sure that you spell-check everything before you submit the self-tape.

Slates take us back to the opening of the book—finding your truth and sticking to it. You should identify something about yourself that you can share with casting directors if they meet you in person or via Zoom. This is a job interview, so in the slate you should self-present professionally and formally. If you are playing a preppy sorority girl, perhaps your slate should be a little cheery and upbeat. If you are auditioning for a play about the Vietnam War, perhaps your slate could have a bit of reserve. In all cases, your slate should fit the mood of the scene and feel inviting to the casting director so that they want to meet you.

Love and believe in yourself, and put your best version of you forward in the slate. Be natural and not "active" or "fake" because casting directors can smell drama and malarkey a mile away. You can't fool them; they do this for a living. If you come with baggage, they will see it, even when you think you are hiding everything.

Technically, make sure you have not only your audition sides recorded but also profile, closeup (chest to head only), and full-body shots of yourself. You may consider asking your agent or manager about separating your audition from your slate in separate digital files. Some people will direct you to do your slate first on your self-tape, but more and more casting directors do not have time to watch your stats and introduction up front and want to see the scene right away. Ask your agent or the casting agency if they want to receive the self-tape with or without slates.

If you want to get a feel for self-tapes, there are many free workshops by working casting directors on YouTube. Many hold master classes monthly and share insights about the things they like to see in self-tape practices. The exciting thing about the self-tape culture is that casting directors have the opportunity to review a past tape that you submitted and did not book for a new project that they are casting. Believe that most casting directors are cheering for you. Whether your casting director is nice, supportive, microaggressive, unprofessional, or bitter, do not let any of this deter you from doing the work. This will be easier if you establish healthy boundaries and a wellness plan. Also, if a casting director says anything that is offensive to your identity, report it. You do not have to take it up with them directly in the room unless you want to. There is no need to leave a casting director with information that they can potentially use against you. You can report inappropriate behavior anonymously to the Casting Society of America.

REELS

Reels should be sent to casting directors on request or on general inquiries. Casting directors do not have time to look at all of the performances on your reel. You should keep your reel up to date with quality performances no longer than two minutes total. If you do not have a reel that is put together from various booked jobs, think about recording a self-tape with an excellent monologue to have ready in case your agent asks for a tape to submit you for general meetings with casting directors or others.

COSTUMES AND PROPS

For the most part, you will not want to wear a costume in auditions, but you do want to pay attention to the role and "look" the part to the best of your ability. Try not to be distracting. If you are playing a teacher, a shirt and sweater will suffice. You can use colors, textures, and tones to relay the energy needed in the scene. Use props sparingly. Cell phones are acceptable, but otherwise, unless the prop is integral to the action of the scene, try to use gestures. By no means should you bring a prop weapon to the audition or record it in a self-tape. In the case of props for self-tapes and live auditions, less is more.

SELF-TAPE RECAP

1. Do as many takes as you need to get the best version of you telling the story as the character.
2. Pay attention to the details. Identify and map your truth, story, punctuation, historical and cultural context clues, stereotypes, and mapping of your script. See yourself in the story, and make it plain that you know what you are doing in the scene to produce the desired emotions. Simple and clean are better than busy and messy.
3. Remember that casting directors are human resources agents. They have to find people for the job or they don't get paid. Be an excellent job candidate so that they will remember you and get you placed on a job. You have to show yourself as a skilled and competent artist who is prepared to do the job. Do this work for yourself, and you'll be not only called in for the audition but also called back for the job.

10

AGENTS AND MANAGERS

There are many ways to get an agent or manager, but first you have to ask yourself, "Am I ready?" This question takes us back to our opening discussion about truth. After reading this book, we hope you are now entering a space where you can tell yourself the truth about your talent, preparedness, ability, and work ethic. It may sound simple, but most people stay in a delusional state about their talent and work ethic for many years and find themselves blaming their career failures on an agent or manager who "didn't do their job." The more important question is: "Did you do yours?"

There is a reason why agents and managers are entitled to only a percentage of your earned income: they only do a percentage of the 100 percent effort that it takes to *help* move you from aspiring to working as an actor. The rest of the work is on you. In most mainstream and regional markets, industry standard is to take 10 to 15 percent of your earnings. Manager percentages vary by practitioners and range from 10 to 30 percent.

So what do we mean by "The rest of the work is on you"? The simple answer is that you are the one who has to create and execute the vision plan for your career. You are the one who has to improve your skillsets. You are in charge of having materials that reflect industry needs and demands. You can create opportunities that align

with your goals. Before you solicit representation, you need to prepare the tools that they require.

REQUIRED MATERIALS

Headshots

You must have a clear and current set of headshots: theatrical (not
smiling), commercial (smiling), and full body (usually provided on
request). Outside light or studio framing to mimic outside light is
preferred. Check out reputable Los Angeles and New York photog-
raphers' websites to see which styles are trending.

All headshots should be in color, and you should have a high-
quality JPEG available to submit yourself. If you can afford it, make
sure that you hire a makeup artist and hair stylist who understands
headshot photography and your skin tones and hair texture. The
picture should look exactly like you, but better. Do not wear heavy
makeup or dress up like you're going to a formal. Consider having a
consultation with the photographer and makeup artist before you
shoot to make sure you have a fit. If you cannot afford to hire
professionals, copy headshots of artists in your same age group and
type. What did they wear? How was their makeup? What was the
light like? If their headshots look like amateur Glamour Shots from
the 1980s or your run-of-the-mill senior year photo, disregard this
advice. Nine times out of ten, if you look in Google images at a
recent actor who is "emerging" on stage, TV, or film, you will see
up-to-date marketing materials that reflect the current market standards and needs.

Résumé

Your acting résumé should only have your acting information, not
previous job experiences at any place that has nothing to do with
acting. This includes internships in any other facet of the industry. If

you are an actor, you're an actor. If you also work as a production assistant to pay the bills, then put that experience on another résumé. Casting directors want to know that you are serious about *acting*. You can easily download actor résumé templates. Including a small headshot on the back of your résumé is a nice touch. Basic bio information is essential: name, agent or self-representation contact information, height (weight is often asked), and hair and eye color. You should include information about your training, skills, languages, accents and dialects, and other performance areas in order of mastery, capacity, and fluency.

SOCIAL MEDIA AND WEB PRESENCE

Many actors are foregoing websites now due to actor presence on social media. You have more daily interaction with the entertainment community on Instagram, Snapchat, and Facebook and new platforms like CreateEnsemble for emerging and established artists. Having a website imprint is a good landing page for your social media presence. As you reach out to agents and managers for representation, your website is a place where they can easily locate your reel, headshots, résumé, and other information about your performances (theater, film, and television) that you can chronicle on a blog on your site. Wix.com and Wordpress.com, among others, are sites that you can use to make your website. We advise you to secure the URL and usernames of the name you will use as an actor. This URL purchase (we also suggest Instagram and Twitter handles connected to your name) is an incredibly important step as you advance in your career. There is a whole industry dedicated to purchasing and reselling URLs that may be valuable to people, and the more famous you become, the more expensive your URL. Buying yours now may save you a great deal of money in the long run.

As far as your social media presence, now is the time to be careful with what you post. Casting directors are employers. If your social media presence is disturbing, and by that we mean you post sexually explicit material, violence, or drug content, clean up your web presence before you reach out because like it or not, people do judge. You can have a social media account that is private and one that is public to distinguish your professional and personal lives.

Once you have your marketing tools, you are prepared to reach out to agents. If you do not have any experience, there really is no need to reach out. Hold until you feel you have enough experience to do what casting directors will expect of you.

REACHING OUT TO AGENTS

When you reach out to agents, you should know something about them and their work. Do they have talent in your category? If so, how many? What level is the agent? Do they only represent working actors? Emerging talent? If you expect to book the top agents who represent household names, that is an unrealistic expectation. This is not to say that you will not be represented by those agencies in the future, but setting realistic goals is key for your success.

Do your research. You can spend years with an agent or manager who is just getting their foot in the door and may not be able to get you the auditions that you want. You can have a candid business conversation with your agent or potential agent. You should have completed homework on the agent or manager before you get to the in-person meeting or Zoom meeting. Please don't waste time asking agents and managers questions whose answers can be found online. Here are some simple questions for your meeting:

1. How many years have you been an agent? (You can actually look this one up if the agent is well known.)
2. How many actors of my type do you represent in my age group?
3. What qualities do I have that you think are important?
4. How would you pitch me to casting directors?
5. How do you prefer your talent to engage with you? Email? Text? Phone?

6. How long will my contract be, and what percentage will you take of bookings? Will you take your percentage pre-tax?
7. Are my materials excellent enough to give you the best tools to pitch me as a talent?
8. Do you have recommendations for my headshots or reel, or are you satisfied with my materials at this time?

Make sure you interview your agent with as much invested in them as you expect them to invest in you. Just because an agent says they want to represent you does not mean that they are a good fit for you. You should seek out a mutually beneficial arrangement. In any case, having an agent makes you more attractive to other agents. You can always try out an agent and then leave, provided you have properly reviewed the termination clause in your contract and given proper notice. We suggest running all contracts past an attorney to make sure you understand the financial and logistical promises you are signing off on. Remember, treat people how you want to be treated. If you are a bridge burner, don't be surprised when casting directors and agents don't want to work with you. The information grapevine is real in entertainment. Do not underestimate the power of a great impression and excellent manners.

Just like you are passionate about your craft as an actor, agents are also passionate about their work. Agents and managers want talent who are professional, know what they are doing, and have a sense of where they fit into the needs or voids of the marketplace. They want actors who will show up and do what they say they can do on their résumé. So, as discussed in chapter 2, tell the truth. Do not lie. If you cannot roller skate, do not put it on your résumé. If you do not speak Spanish, do not put it on your résumé. It's simple. Be honest about who you are and where you are, lean into your truth, and you will present the best version of yourself that you can on your self-tape or live audition.

When you write to an agent via email, Instagram, Facebook, or other social media outlets to ask for a general meeting, tell the truth. Tell them why they are the person to take a risk on you. Show them that you know who they are and what they have done. If you know talent that they have discovered in your category, tell them. Make the connection between your talent and work ethic with the type of talent that they represent. If you do not hear back right away, follow up. Look at their social media and see what interests them even before you reach out. Check out their IMDb page to see what shows or films they have cast. Look at Playbill.com or Broadway.com to see what plays they have cast. Have the information you need to make a lasting first impression. You should know why you want to explore the possibility of working with them beyond a general desire to have an agent.

ABOUT FACE

Have a poker face. Do not let folks see you sweat. Stay encouraged, and do not give up if you do not get a response right away. Find the agent's or manager's address, and send them an invite or comp tickets to see a play you are in. Send an old-fashioned postcard, and let them know when you book a commercial or a television show guest spot. No matter where you're coming from in your career, you must give yourself credibility and lead with that when talking about your work in the industry. For someone just starting out, you can get quotes from your acting teachers praising your work and post them on your website along with the best self-tape you can produce. Log what works for you and what doesn't. Once you get a few breakthroughs, you will be able to track your communication practices and hone them for future career outreach work.

If you are someone who has booked theater, TV, or film roles, let casting directors know the shows and what you learned from the process. For example, "My recent guest star on *Westworld* [(2016) created by Jonathan Nolan and Lisa Joy] gave me valuable experience working in multi-camera shoots. Working with a veteran performer like Thandie Newton allowed me to really understand the value of supporting roles." Using these types of enlivening details about your acting roles will really make your email inquiries for face-to-face meetings stand out from the many email and analog paper inquiries agents and managers receive.

GET TO THE POINT

Agents and managers are very busy. Actually, everyone is busy in life, so value the time of people who you reach out to for help. If you want to have an informational meeting about what you will need to be considered by the agency, say that. If you want the opportunity to send a self-tape or to go in for a read for consideration, before you ask anything, go to the agency's website and see what the requirements are for meetings or solicitations. Some larger agencies will not take unsolicited self-submissions. It is counterproductive to put in all the work of crafting your tools and outreach emails to send to a company that does not even consider cold calls. Emails are statistically proven to be answered more frequently when the subject line and content are concise and to the point of what you want. Be polite and considerate. If you do not know how to write a proper letter, email, or thank-you card, buy an etiquette book or search templates online. Kindness and compassion go a long way. Entertainment is business; it is not personal. No one has time for foolishness, so present yourself professionally and leave a good impression.

KNOW YOUR TYPE

Make sure you clearly articulate what types of roles you are often cast in or would be going out for. We tell actors to identify two working actors who people say they resemble and use that to pitch themselves: "I'm a cross between Eva Longoria and Jennifer Lopez. I have worked primarily in ingénue roles." This is a helpful context, but you have to live up to the pitch. If you do not look like Eva or Jennifer, you are wasting the time of the agent or manager. They can see your photos, so it should not be a shock if you do not get a call after you misrepresent your looks or other characteristics. You can replicate these same tips for reaching out to casting directors.

Here are a few helpful hints as to what you can include in your outreach correspondence:

- Link to your professional casting accounts at ActorsAccess.com and CastingFrontier.com (for a commercial).
- Link to your website with your reel, headshots, and résumé.
- If you do not have a website, have a PDF and JPEG of your headshot and a link to your reel parked on your YouTube channel or platform like CreateEnsemble.

Let your personality shine throughout your email. Spell-check everything. Your misspelled words tell the agent, manager, or casting director that details are not your strong suit. Find the agents and managers who are accepting new clients, and see where your skillsets fit their needs. Realize that agents and managers are very busy. Try not to take it personally if you do not receive an answer to your correspondence right away. We suggest going onto agency and manager websites and social media to identify the assistants of the people you're trying to reach. Sometimes, you can make a lot of headway with the gatekeepers by inviting them to your events, briefing them about your appearances, and liking their social media posts in respectful ways.

FOLLOW-UP

There is a fine line between follow-up and harassment. Mark a calendar or spreadsheet with the date of your first outreach to each agent or manager. Save all of your correspondence in a folder so that you know what you said and what feedback you received. Think about following up every eight to ten weeks or so. Pace yourself. You do not want to be blocked on social media or placed on a "do not respond" list because you are overdoing outreach and follow-up messages. Follow normal business protocols, as you would for any business decision. Again, these same outreach strategies can be used for casting directors.

Backstage (a trade publication for actors and other entertainment professionals) has a digital list of agencies (for agents and managers) that you can search for by city and state. Most agencies will tell you if they are looking for new talent. If you have a friend or associate who has seen your work and given you favorable reviews, you can ask them if they would feel comfortable referring you to their agent. This would involve your contact writing an email introduction or arranging for an in-person meeting. Another option is to make certain that all of your material is up to date when you perform in plays, TV shows, or films so that you can post your performance dates and tag agencies that are looking for talent in your type group on social media.

As an actor of the global majority, it is important that you think about galvanizing your follower base on social media as an "added value" that you bring to discussion tables. If you have more than five thousand followers on Instagram, you are bringing a built-in audience base with you, and this is valuable to talent agents and managers who are trying to market new talent to producers and directors.

Polishing and shining your talent, craft, and marketing materials puts you in a winning position when opportunities present themselves. Invest the money and time to "buy once" with high-quality materials so that you won't be sent to the drawing board once again. You are worth your investment. Tuning in to your physical, mental, spiritual, and intellectual well-being as an actor is part of taking care of your instrument. This is why we tell you that half the battle of acting, auditioning, and booking jobs is telling the truth. If your truth is in sync with the best version of you, you will identify the best qualities of your character and be able to hone in on their truth.

Once you have a clear breakdown about who you are, breaking down your scripts and mapping a thoughtful and informed choice that demonstrates talent, skill, and preparation, no one will be able to stop you on your journey. Systemic barriers that persist are real, yet your awareness of them can better equip you to surmount them.

You are an amazing artist who can and will do many great things. We want you to hear that and believe it no matter what the industry projects about people of the global majority. Take all of the good that you have and that there is in the industry and use it as your personal stepping stone to get to where you want to go. Give yourself and your craft the love, discipline, and inspiration you need to be the best actor you can be. There is no one to compete with besides yourself. There is room for everyone. There is no obstacle that actors of the global majority who came before you have not overcome. Stand strong in yourself, and know that with these fundamental audition skills, you have what it takes to break it down, bring it, and book the job.

TEN-STEP BREAKING-IT-DOWN PLAN—JOURNAL PROMPTS

1. **Boundaries and wellness plan:** Spend time identifying your personal boundaries so that you know what you will and will not do in an audition. Write them down and stick to them. Book appointments with yourself to do the work on your calendar.
2. **Tell the truth:** Know who you are and what you want. If you can't tell your truth, how do you expect to play the truth of your character? Make post-its, mantras, or digital prompts to remind you of your truth.
3. **Read the story:** We can't say this enough: read the story. Reading the story a minimum of five times immerses you in the world of the play, TV show, or film as set forth in those few audition pages. See, feel, touch the world in the story, and the lines will come because you will know the who, what, when, where, and why of the story in the scene at hand. Write down what the story is in one sentence and memorize it.
4. **Play the punctuation and practice pronunciation:** Punctuation tells you how the line is said and how the writer imagines its pacing and tone. Keep in mind that punctuation us-

age and pronunciation shifts between Western and non-Western languages, so make the appropriate adjustments. Understand all of your punctuation mark definitions so that you can translate those moments into your performance. To run over or ignore punctuation is to miss part of the line as written. Write a Post-it to remind yourself before auditions.

5. **Play the action:** Playing action in- and outside of Stanislavskian acting approaches simply means asking, *What am I doing in the scene?* and *What do I want?* Whatever you are *doing* is the *action* you are playing as it relates to whatever emotional state the characters are in.

6. **Identify emotions:** Identify all of the emotional cues in the scene descriptions, parentheticals, and dialogue for any of the characters. These clues help you establish the tone of the performance and the product of the action. Writing these down helps you get them in your body.

7. **Identify historical and cultural contexts:** Historical and cultural context clues are vital to understanding how the character's identity is positioned with the story. We encourage you to think through and write down all context clues from an intersectional standpoint. You cannot separate parts of your character's identity. They all work together.

8. **Face stereotypes:** Stereotypes are part of life. Do we like them? No. Should we be very much aware of them? Absolutely. If you consent to play a stereotype, just own it and subvert it the best you can. If you choose to subvert the stereotype by attempting to reconfirm the archetype in some way, do that. If you can't handle stereotypes that you read in the audition sides at all, decline to audition. Don't waste your time or the casting director's time auditioning for roles you know you will never take.

9. **Self-tape security:** Invest in the materials that you need to make a great self-tape. Self-taping is the way that almost 85 percent of casting directors operate now, so welcome to your future. You can improvise a home studio with found items and textures. For example, you could use a gray poster board

as a self-tape background for less than $1. You can self-tape in natural light. Be creative and follow the directions.

10. **Agents and managers dos and don'ts:** Present your best and most professional self when reaching out to agents, managers, or casting directors. You cannot undo a first impression gone wrong, so make sure that what people are seeing is what you hope they will see in the future.

CONCLUSION

As actors of the global majority, we have to face these truths and empower ourselves with the knowledge to boldly claim space and to lift our voices to do what we must to work in this industry. Setting clear boundaries that center your wellness and telling the truth in healthy and productive ways about who you are and what you stand for in any field is important. Developing and sharpening your skills can go a long way in enabling you to walk fully in your purpose as you pursue a career in acting. Seek out teachers who can help you gain the skills that you need to claim. No matter how good we become, we can always benefit from sharpening our skills at every level of excellence.

As you prepare for your next audition, approach it like you are applying for a job to work with a creative team that is truly invested in truthfully telling stories grounded in the humanity of the range of communities your body/instrument and skillsets can represent. Recognize that due to historical inequity and bias, this is not always the case for actors of the global majority. This is not right and needs to change. We believe it can change through collective resistance, dismantling and rebuilding with equity and empathy, and affirming one another through truthful storytelling. Your approach to your formal or informal training and cultivated craft for auditions and booked roles is all part of the larger goal of changing the system. If we collectively refuse to traffic in stereotypes and the dehumanization of the people and cultures our bodies represent and embrace the opportunities that align with the objective of portraying the greatest range and depth of humanity, the system cannot stand as it is.

Entering the room with knowledge of self and the ways your body and skills can contribute to storytelling that reflects the depth and range of the people and communities you are called on to represent is one of many steps you can take as an individual and as a part of this collective resistance. This can shift the very foundations of the industry we work in through grassroots efforts even as we work to restructure and reform throughout. So, remember, we are not powerless. Once we collectively recognize our individual and collective power, the greatest change can come. And as it does, we must be ready.

Recognize and hone your skills so when the time comes to tell our stories, you are prepared to do so as we take care of ourselves and one another in the process. At the end of the day, it all begins with you and the outgrowth you produce in your daily life and your work.

Trying to impress those who do not recognize your humanity at the outset can be soul killing. When you, your loved ones, and those who embrace your humanity are the audience you imagine when you enter an audition rather than those who may be in positions of power, you will be more likely to achieve the depth and nuance you aspire to in performing any given role. For many performance traditions emanating from the cultures of people of the global majority, there is no separation between performer and audience. This is why it can feel so heavy to take on stereotypical roles even if we subvert them and experience criticism from our communities.

Even as the written text serves as your point of departure, let your imagined audiences play a healthy role in how you approach the work. It's not about people-pleasing in role selection, audition strategy, or performance. It's about embracing the reality that we are all connected, and that many of us are intimately connected to our communities. Just like W. E. B. Du Bois's idea of double consciousness, navigating how the industry often sees people of the global majority and how we see ourselves as worthy and amazingly talented people doesn't have to be a burden when you use it as a superpower. Double consciousness can be viewed as a gift of "second sight" that enables us to see the industry and systems of inequality for what they are. We can subvert the negative aspects by learning our craft and telling the truth in our work and about how we are treated.

So often people of the global majority are told that we "are lucky" to be a part of a production or that we "can't say anything" about mistreatment. If we do not tell the truth about the work when we are performing and in our work conditions, no matter who treats us inappropriately, including other industry professionals of color, then we are perpetuating the same systems that hurt us. Our communities can be the incubated spaces that nurture and embolden us as artists by ordaining us as truth tellers and pushing us to tell the truth in our work. How we show up matters. So be sure to show up as you, in all your glory, and as the character in the performance.

So, once you set healthy boundaries and establish a wellness plan that puts you first, you are better positioned to break down the audition process rather than being broken down by the process itself. You can take each step toward "bringing it" and bringing "you" into the audition and booking the job. The rest will be up to you. So stay encouraged and walk in your purpose. We are rooting for you! Remember the three Bs: Break it down! Bring it! Book it!

Best,
Nicole and Monica

APPENDIX

Actor Training Resources: Alternatives and Supplements to Eurocentric Approaches

The historical narrative of actor training has thus far been limited to predominantly White accounts of Eurocentric training programs. Documenting the history of training for actors of color has been almost nonexistent. Many scholars and practitioners have addressed the ways actor training by artists and scholars of the global majority has been largely erased from actor-training history. The resource list included in this book offers a mere snapshot of theater companies, studios, and university programs that produce training programs and classes for artists of the global majority that are rooted in their cultural and racial experiences. For supplemental resources for auditioning, visit BreakingItDownBook.com for access to our PDFs for extended journal prompts, spreadsheet templates to track auditions, wellness plan templates, and other resources.

Supplemental Stanislavsky-Based and Non-Eurocentric Techniques Developed by African American Actor Trainers

- The Black Arts Institute
- The CRAFT Institute
- Black Acting Methods Studio
- Sylvan Baker, Applied Theatre (UK)
- Nicole Brewer, Anti-Racist Theatre
- Kashi Johnson, hip-hop acting methods
- Will Power, hip-hop theatre approaches
- Tasha Smith, Actor's Studio, Atlanta
- Black Theatre Commons—HowlRound
- Latinx Theatre Commons—HowlRound
- Waco Theatre Center—Los Angeles
- Baron Kelly, Acting Approach

Non-Eurocentric Acting at Colleges and Universities

- University of Louisville
- Brown University
- Norfolk State University
- Clark Atlanta University
- Spelman College
- Howard University
- University of Wisconsin–Madison
- Tennessee State University
- Kentucky State University
- Claflin University
- Winston Salem State University
- University of Miami (Ohio)
- Simmons College
- Florida Agricultural Mechanical University

Theatres of the Global Majority with Actor Training Opportunities (Select List)

- The Negro Ensemble Theatre
- The New Federal Theatre
- The National Black Theatre
- The Billie Holiday Theatre
- North Carolina Black Repertory Theatre
- St. Louis Black Repertory Theatre
- Kansas City Black Repertory Theatre
- Penumbra Theatre
- Jubilee Theatre
- Encore Theatre
- ProArts Collective
- Hi-Arts
- The Black Academy of Arts and Letters
- DNA Works
- Hattiloo Theatre
- KC Melting Pot Theatre
- Crossroads Theatre
- East West Players
- Native Voices at the Autry
- Obsidian Theater
- The Ensemble Theater
- Plowshares Theater
- Penumbra Theater
- Deaf Spotlight
- Teatrx—Houston
- Repertorio Espagñol
- Golden Thread Theatre Company
- CATS (Contemporary Asian Theatre Scene)
- New Federal Theatre
- Asian Pacific Islander Cultural Center
- New Native Theatre
- Spiderwoman Theatre
- Splitbritches Theatre

- Vision Theatre—Los Angeles
- WACO Theater Center - Los Angeles

Actor-Friendly Websites

- Actors Access
- Actor Pad
- Backstage
- Playbill
- Now Casting
- LA Casting
- NY Casting
- Casting Frontier
- Casting Networks
- CreateEnsemble

Social Media Resources

- Reddit Actor
- Daily Actor
- Black Acting Methods
- Inside the Actor Studio Apartment
- B.A.B.E.
- Shadow and Act
- Broadway Black
- Blacktress UK
- The Undefeated
- Black Actors Page (Facebook)
- Nosotros (Facebook)
- HOLA Hispanic Federation of Latin Actors (Facebook)
- Native American Actors (Facebook)
- Native American Casting (Facebook)
- Asian American Actors (Facebook)
- Arab American Actors (Facebook)
- Asian Americans and Pacific Islanders on TV (Facebook)

- Stage Milk

Academic Articles and Books about Actor Training by Educators of the Global Majority

- Kaja Dunn, Sharrell D. Luckett, and Daphne Sicre, "Training Theatre Students of Colour in the United States," *Theatre, Dance and Performance Training* 11, no. 3 (2020): 274–82.
- Sharrell Luckett and Tia Shaffer, *Black Acting Methods: Critical Approaches* (New York: Routledge, 2016).
- Omi Osun and Joni L. Jones, *Theatrical Jazz: Performance, Àse, and the Power of the Present Moment* (Columbus: The Ohio State University Press, 2015).
- Monica White Ndounou, *Shaping the Future of African American Film: Color-Coded Economics and the Story Behind the Numbers* (New Brunswick, NJ: Rutgers University Press, 2014).
- Monica White Ndounou, "Being Black on Stage and Screen: Black Actor Training before Black Power and the Rise of Stanislavski's System." In *The Routledge Companion to African American Theatre and Performance*, ed. A. Perkins Kathy, L. Richards Sandra, Alexander Craft Renée, and F. DeFrantz Thomas (London: Routledge, 2018).

NOTES

INTRODUCTION

1. Howard University, "Chadwick Boseman's Howard University 2018 Commencement Speech," YouTube, May 14, 2018, video, 34:40, www.youtube.com/watch?v=RIHZypMyQ2s.

2. Jacob Shamsian and Tom Murray, "Chadwick Boseman Recalled Being Fired from a TV Show after Questioning the Racial Stereotypes of His Role," *Insider*, August 29, 2020, www.insider.com/chadwick-boseman-fired-tv-show-question-black-stereotypes-2018-5.

3. SAG/AFTRA Talk on Race YouTube.

4. PGM One: People of the Global Majority in the Outdoors, Nature, & Environment, "Home," accessed December 3, 2020, www.pgmone.org.

5. Actors' Equity Association, "Looking at Hiring Biases by the Numbers," *Equity News*, Spring 2017, 8–18, https://actorsequity.org/news/EquityNews/Spring2017/en_02_2017.pdf#page=5; Darnell Hunt, Ana-Christina Ramón, and Michael Tran, *Hollywood Diversity Report 2019: Old Story, New Beginning* (UCLA College Social Sciences, 2019), https://socialsciences.ucla.edu/wp-content/uploads/2019/02/UCLA-Hollywood-Diversity-Report-2019-2-21-2019.pdf.

I. ESTABLISHING AND BREAKING BOUNDARIES

1. Kimberlé Crenshaw, "Mapping the Margins: Intersectionality, Identity Politics, and Violence against Women of Color," *Stanford Law Review* 43, no. 6 (July 1991): 1241–99; Patricia Hill Collins, *Intersectionality as Critical Social Theory* (Durham, NC: Duke University Press, 2019).

2. TELL THE TRUTH

1. "Gone with the Wind (1939)," The Numbers, accessed December 3, 2020, www.the-numbers.com/movie/Gone-with-the-Wind#tab=summary.

3. READ THE STORY, NOT THE LINES

1. Konstantin Stanislavsky, *An Actor Prepares* (New York: Theatre Arts, 1946).

4. PLAY PUNCTUATION AND PRACTICE PRONUNCIATION

1. Ntozake Shange, "Unrecovered Losses/Black Theater Traditions," *The Black Scholar* 10, no. 10 (July/August 1979): 7–9.

2. We highly recommend Paul Meier's International Dialects of English Archive: www.dialectsarchive.com. IDEA is one of the only archives of primary-source recordings of English-language dialects and accents from around the world.

3. Lena Waithe, "*Twenties*: 'Pilot,'" accessed December 8, 2020, https://thetelevisionpilot.com/wp-content/uploads/2020/04/Twenties_1x01_-_Pilot.pdf.

4. Ted Shine, *Contribution*, in *Black Theatre USA*, vol. 2 (New York: The Free Press, 1996).

5. Langston Hughes, *Limitations of Life* (New York: New Theatre League, 1939).

6. Langston Hughes, *The Collected Works of Langston Hughes*, vol. 5, ed. Leslie Catherine Sanders and Nancy Johnston (Columbia: University of Missouri Press, 2002), 583.

7. Pete Nowalk, "*How to Get Away with Murder*: 'Pilot,'" accessed December 9, 2020, www.zen134237.zen.co.uk/How_To_Get _Away_With_Murder_1x01_-_Pilot.pdf.

8. Suzan-Lori Parks, *The America Play and Other Works* (New York: Theatre Communications Group, 1996).

9. Lorraine Hansberry, *A Raisin in the Sun*, in *Black Theatre USA*, vol. 2 (New York: The Free Press, 1996), 140.

10. Alice Childress, *Wine in the Wilderness*, in *Black Theatre USA*, vol. 2 (New York: The Free Press, 1996).

11. Childress, *Wine in the Wilderness*.

12. Nowalk, "*How to Get Away with Murder*: 'Pilot.'"

5. PLAYING THE ACTION

1. Konstantin Stanislavsky, *An Actor Prepares* (New York: Theatre Arts, 1946).

2. Jessica B. Harris, "The National Black Theatre: The Sun People of 125th Street," in *The Theatre of Black Americans*, ed. Errol Hill (New York: Applause, 1987), 283; Lundeana Thomas, *Barbara Ann Teer and the National Black Theatre: Transformational Forces in Harlem* (New York: Routledge, 2016).

6. IDENTIFYING THE EMOTIONS

1. At the time of publication many television shows are in flux as the entertainment industry explores best practices to return to work safely. While we are hopeful that many of the shows cited here will survive the COVID-19 crisis, we realize that shows in this volume may be cancelled at the time of publication. We encourage you to seek out streaming episodes of these productions for reference.

2. Lorraine Hansberry, radio interview with Studs Terkel, broadcast on WFMT Radio, Chicago, IL, May 12, 1959, quoted in "Make New Sounds:

Studs Terkel Interviews Lorraine Hansberry," *American Theater* (November 1984): 6.

3. August Wilson, interview with Bill Moyer, 1988, quoted in "Playwright August Wilson on Writing about Black America," Moyers on Democracy, February 25, 2017, https://billmoyers.com/story/august-wilson-on-writing-about-black-america.

8. FACE STEREOTYPES

1. Nancy Wang Yuen, *Reel Inequality: Hollywood Actors and Racism* (New Brunswick, NJ: Rutgers University Press, 2016); Kristen J. Warner, *The Cultural Politics of Colorblind TV Casting* (New York: Routledge, 2015).

9. SELF-TAPES

1. SAG-AFTRA, "Casting Directors Dish Self-Tape Tips," September 13, 2019, www.sagaftra.org/casting-directors-dish-self-tape-tips.

2. We suggest you looking at the YouTube channels of many casting directors to get tips on self-tapes. Some of our favorites resources include interviews from Inside Black Actors Studio, Cody Beke, Amy Jo Berman, Tracy "Twinkie" Byrd, Leah Daniels Butler, Kahleen Crawford, Carmen Cuba, Amy Lenker Doyle, Barbara Fiorintino, Amy Lyndon, Sarah Finn, Sarah Halley, Carla Hool, Lori Opended, John Papsidera, and Robi Reed. Also check out other casting directors who have a history of giving breaks to talent of color. Breakdown services, CastIt, Actor Access, Casting Networks, Backstage, Spotlight, IMDbPro, and other emerging casting platforms are all used by casting directors to find talent. You should get any access that you can to these systems, because casting directors are using them to access actors globally.

BIBLIOGRAPHY

Actors' Equity Association. "Looking at Hiring Biases by the Numbers." *Equity News*, Spring 2017, 8–18. https://actorsequity.org/news/EquityNews/Spring2017/en_02_2017.pdf#page=5.

Childress, Alice. *Wine in the Wilderness*. In *Black Theatre USA*, vol. 2. New York: The Free Press, 1996.

Collins, Patricia Hill. *Intersectionality as Critical Social Theory*. Durham, NC: Duke University Press, 2019.

Crenshaw, Kimberlé. "Mapping the Margins: Intersectionality, Identity Politics, and Violence against Women of Color." *Stanford Law Review* 43, no. 6 (July 1991): 1241–99.

Dunn, Kaja, Sharrell D. Luckett, and Daphne Sicre. "Training Theatre Students of Colour in the United States." *Theatre, Dance and Performance Training* 11, no. 3 (2020): 274–82.

"Gone with the Wind (1939)." The Numbers. Accessed December 3, 2020. www.the-numbers.com/movie/Gone-with-the-Wind#tab=summary.

Hansberry, Lorraine. Radio interview with Studs Terkel. Broadcast on WFMT Radio, Chicago, IL, May 12, 1959. Quoted in "Make New Sounds: Studs Terkel Interviews Lorraine Hansberry." *American Theater* (November 1984): 6.

———. *A Raisin in the Sun*. In *Black Theatre USA*, vol. 2. New York: The Free Press, 1996.

Harris, Jessica B. "The National Black Theatre: The Sun People of 125th Street." In *The Theatre of Black Americans*, edited by Errol Hill, 283–92. New York: Applause, 1987.

Howard University. "Chadwick Boseman's Howard University 2018 Commencement Speech." YouTube. May 14, 2018. Video, 34:40. www.youtube.com/watch?v=RIHZypMyQ2s.

Hughes, Langston. *The Collected Works of Langston Hughes*, vol. 5. Edited by Leslie Catherine Sanders and Nancy Johnston. Columbia: University of Missouri Press, 2002.

———. *Limitations of Life*. New York: New Theatre League, 1939.

Hunt, Darnell, Ana-Christina Ramón, and Michael Tran. *Hollywood Diversity Report 2019: Old Story, New Beginning*. UCLA College Social Sciences, 2019. https://

socialsciences.ucla.edu/wp-content/uploads/2019/02/UCLA-Hollywood-Diversity-Report-2019-2-21-2019.pdf.

Luckett, Sharrell, and Tia Shaffer. *Black Acting Methods: Critical Approaches*. New York: Routledge, 2016.

Ndounou, Monica White. *Acting Your Color: The CRAFT, Power, and Paradox of Acting for Black Americans*. Evanston, IL: Northwestern University Press, forthcoming (2021).

———. *Shaping the Future of African American Film: Color-Coded Economics and the Story Behind the Numbers*. New Brunswick, NJ: Rutgers University Press, 2014.

Nowalk, Pete. *"How to Get Away with Murder*: 'Pilot.'" Accessed December 9, 2020. www.zen134237.zen.co.uk/How_To_Get_Away_With_Murder_1x01_-_Pilot.pdf.

Osun, Omi, and Joni L. Jones. *Theatrical Jazz: Performance, Àse, and the Power of the Present Moment*. Columbus: The Ohio State University Press, 2015.

Parks, Suzan-Lori. *The America Play and Other Works*. New York: Theatre Communications Group, 1996.

PGM One: People of the Global Majority in the Outdoors, Nature, & Environment. "Home." Accessed December 3, 2020. www.pgmone.org.

SAG-AFTRA. "Casting Directors Dish Self-Tape Tips." September 13, 2019. www.sagaftra.org/casting-directors-dish-self-tape-tips.

Shamsian, Jacob, and Tom Murray. "Chadwick Boseman Recalled Being Fired from a TV Show after Questioning the Racial Stereotypes of His Role." *Insider*, August 29, 2020. www.insider.com/chadwick-boseman-fired-tv-show-question-black-stereotypes-2018-5.

Shange, Ntozake. "Unrecovered Losses/Black Theater Traditions." *The Black Scholar* 10, no. 10 (July/August 1979): 7–9.

Shine, Ted. *Contribution*. In *Black Theatre USA*, vol. 2. New York: The Free Press, 1996.

Stanislavsky, Konstantin. *An Actor Prepares*. New York: Theatre Arts, 1946.

Thomas, Lundeana. *Barbara Ann Teer and the National Black Theatre: Transformational Forces in Harlem*. New York: Routledge, 2016.

Waithe, Lena. *"Twenties*: 'Pilot.'" Accessed December 8, 2020. https://thetelevisionpilot.com/wp-content/uploads/2020/04/Twenties_1x01_-_Pilot.pdf.

Warner, Kristen J. *The Cultural Politics of Colorblind TV Casting*. New York: Routledge, 2015.

Wilson, August. Interview with Bill Moyer. 1988. Quoted in "Playwright August Wilson on Writing about Black America." Moyers on Democracy, February 25, 2017. https://billmoyers.com/story/august-wilson-on-writing-about-black-america.

Yuen, Nancy Wang. *Reel Inequality: Hollywood Actors and Racism*. New Brunswick, NJ: Rutgers University Press, 2016.

INDEX

AAVE. *See* African American vernacular English

ableism, xiv, 25, 99, 113

academic articles and books, 147

Academy Awards, 24, 36, 114

accents and dialects: clarity above, 122; pronunciation and, 56; punctuation and, 62; resources for, 150n2; résumé inclusion of skill with, 129; in social and cultural context research, 104, 106; stereotyping and, 112; storytelling role of, 40, 44; tips for handling, 112

action, playing the: in auditions, 79–82, 83; clues and subtext, 80; depth gained in, 79; dialogue connection to, 83; emotional portrayal ties to, 77–78, 79, 82, 86, 88, 90–91, 92, 137; example of, 77; identifying line-by-line, 82; imagination in, 80, 81; journal prompts on, 82–83; listening as, 78; manner of, 81, 88; opening and closing actions importance in auditions, 83, 84; parenthetical information as clues for, 65–67; PGM approaches to, 76; plan for, 41, 78, 80–81, 82, 84, 89; practicing, 80, 84; props and, 80, 83;

spontaneity in, 39; stage business clues about, 47, 89; Stanislavsky on, 38, 75–76, 89; story and prior story understanding in, 43, 80, 81; verb identification and, 80, 84

African American vernacular English (AAVE), x, 51

agency and empowerment: audition confidence with, 18–19, 32, 99, 123, 141; boundaries role in feelings of, 115; preparation impact on, 89; in racial equity work, 139–140; in role selection, ix, 100–101, 115; with self-identity, 14, 89; skills development and, 139; around stereotypes, 13, 24, 101, 109, 111, 113, 114, 115. *See also* self-knowledge and discovery

agents and managers: assistants as contact option, 134; boundaries around roles communicated with, 10, 108; boundaries with, 7–8; conciseness in contact with, 133; contracts, 131; earnings percentage to, 127; failures blamed on, 127; follow-up etiquette, 134–135; interviewing, 25, 130–131; list of, 135; personal truths and honesty

ABOUT THE AUTHORS

Nicole Hodges Persley, PhD, is an associate professor of American studies and African and African American studies at the University of Kansas. She is a courtesy faculty member of the Department of Theatre and Dance. An actress and director, Hodges Persley is a member of SAG/AFTRA/AEA and the SDC (Stage Directors and Choreographers Society). She has performance and directing credits in regional theater, television, and film. Notable directing credits include *A Raisin in the Sun*, *Welcome to Arroyo's*, *Rachel*, *Dutchman*, and *Sunset Baby*. Her forthcoming book, *Sampling and Remixing Blackness in Hip-hop Theater and Performance*, will be published in fall 2021. She has published articles and book chapters on hip-hop theater, hip-hop studies, directing, acting, and Black theater. She is the artistic director of KC Melting Pot Theatre, Kansas City's premier Black theater company. She is a co-founder of CreateEnsemble, a social media platform for creative artists of color.

Monica White Ndounou, PhD, is an associate professor of theater and the 2017–2018 Sony Music Fellow at Dartmouth College. She is the founding member of the National Advisory Committee for The Black Seed and the founding executive director of The CRAFT Institute as well as the award-winning author of *Shaping the Future of African American Film: Color-Coded Economics and the Story* *behind the Numbers.* Also an actor, director, and member of the SDC (Stage Directors and Choreographers Society), her notable directing credits include *Pass Over, Gem of the Ocean, for colored girls who have considered suicide/when the rainbow is enuf,* and *Joe Turner's Come and Gone.* Her forthcoming book, *Acting Your Color: The Craft, Power and Paradox of Acting for Black Americans 1950s to the Present,* is part of a multi-media project that includes a documentary film and digital archive. She is a co-founder of CreateEnsemble, a social media platform for creative artists of color.